Revised Edition

Patricia King

Contents

Introduction	A Prophetic Overview	7
Lesson One	The Cross and the Covenant	15
Lesson Two	New Creation Realities	23
Lesson Three	The Person of the Holy Spirit	29
Lesson Four	Faith: The Connector to Heavenly Glory	39
Lesson Five	The Word of God: Our Basis for Experience	43
Lesson Six	The Rewards of Holiness	45
Lesson Seven	Daily Disciplines for Experiencing Heavenly Glory	53
Lesson Eight	Spiritual Mapping: Mapping the Throne Zone	57
Lesson Nine	Hearing the Voice of God	65
Lesson Ten	Experiencing the Third Heaven Part One	67
Lesson Eleven	Experiencing the Third Heaven Part Two	81
Lesson Twelve	Angelic Majesties	93
Lesson Thirteen	The Fire	99
Lesson Fourteen	The Glory	105
Lesson Fifteen	Heavenly Provision	109
Appendix	"Nuts, Flakes, and Weirdos"	115

The Glory School - Revised Edition

Copyright © 2010 – Patricia King

All rights reserved. This book is protected by the copyright laws of the United States of America. No part of this publication may be reproduced, stored in a retrieval system or transmitted in any form or by any means – electronic, mechanical, photocopy, recording or any other – except for brief quotations, without the prior permission of the author.

Unless otherwise identified, Scripture quotations are from the New American Standard Bible®, Copyright © 1960,1962,1963,1968, 1971,1972,1973,1975,1977,1995 by The Lockman Foundation. Used by permission.

Published by XP Publishing
A department of Christian Services Association
P.O. Box 1017
Maricopa, Arizona 85139
www.XPpublishing.com

Printed in Canada

ISBN-13: 978-1-936101-18-4
ISBN-10: 1-936101-18-1

FROM THE DESK OF
PATRICIA KING

Dear Student,

The Kingdom of heaven is so very rich and full of your Savior's love. You, as God's child, are invited to explore its height, length, depth and breadth through the ministry of His Holy Spirit.

This course is designed to acquaint you with the truth of God's Word concerning who you are in Christ and what wonderful benefits have been granted to you as a believer in Him. You are able to access the throne of grace by faith and enjoy the very presence of God. You are invited to lay hold of every spiritual blessing in the heavenly places in Christ. He loves and adores you!

May this course equip you to be a solid, hungry, passionate and fulfilled believer in Christ. May you grow through this teaching to be one who worships and adores Him with all that is within you. Bless you as you embark on a faith adventure.

Are you ready? Are you hungry? How hungry? Do you desire to be introduced to truth that will enable you to soar in His awesome goodness? Are you desiring to know the Holy Spirit in a personal way? Are you desiring to be a passionate worshipper of Jesus Christ? You are? Good! The Lord will not disappoint you.

Imbibe and enjoy!

Joyful in serving you,

Patricia King

INTRODUCTION

A Prophetic Overview

A New Spiritual Era

All around us today we see people increasingly intrigued by and hungry for spiritual things. An emphasis on materialism, career, and education in our society has, for the most part, left the masses feeling empty and longing for purpose in life. The youth of today are generally fearful of the future and yet are longing to give themselves to something meaningful. They often feel powerless next to the shakings around them.

As a result, the masses are turning to a variety of things that they hope will grant them a sense of security. Some have turned to drugs in an attempt to experience either a feeling of empowerment or an illusive rest from all the pressures that invade their peace. The drug scene with its smorgasbord of choices has left many in this generation broken, disillusioned, and without hope.

Others are attempting to find their well-being through sexual fulfillment. Sexual promiscuity and confusion in sexual orientation have increased greatly in these days, partly due to the fact that people are longing for deep and meaningful relationships. Instead of this goal and desire being realized, many have been left shipwrecked, wounded and violated.

This generation is seeking for something they can live for – something they can die for. Education, family, career, material security, sexual

Introduction Notes

fulfillment, church life, and escapism through the drug scene have all fallen short in satisfying the deep inner cries resident in most hungry hearts. As a result, we are seeing a growing emergence of spiritual hunger and awakening.

SIGNS OF THIS TRANSITION ARE EVERYWHERE

Consequently, we have now entered an era of transition. Signs of this transition are everywhere. Many books and movies today have a spiritual theme. The music industry is promoting sounds of the spirit world. New Age doctrine has infiltrated the education system, the medical profession, the political realm, and the business world. Spiritual superheroes are being introduced through the media, drawing affections and imaginations towards deliverers who promise release and relief. Children's programs, cartoons, and games are often supernatural in nature. Satanic, occult, and New Age groups are growing dramatically as they continue to introduce hungry new converts to the spirit world. Where is the church in the midst of this counterfeit uprising?

Over the years, I have witnessed a great deal of fear and resistance in the body of Christ concerning spiritual language and supernatural activation and experience. It is imperative at this critical hour that we dedicate ourselves afresh to seeking the face of the Lord and to becoming familiar with scriptural teaching concerning the spirit realm. It is vital that we allow the Holy Spirit to lead us into heavenly perspectives that we possibly have not been comfortable with up to this time.

Some of these insights will be introduced initially with a measure of wrestling and resistance in the hearts of believers. We need to learn to discern. In John 3:12, Jesus was speaking to Nicodemus, a ruler of the Jews, saying, "If I told you earthly things and you do not believe, how will you believe if I tell you heavenly things." We will be hearing increased numbers of testimonies regarding believers engaging in spiritual experiences such as those we read about in the Bible. Appearances of Jesus, angelic visitation, traveling in the realm of the spirit, throne room experiences, dreams, visions, trances, and miracles, signs and wonders will be occurring much more frequently.

There are spiritual insights that will be introduced to the church in the coming days that up to this time our "eye has not seen and ear has not heard, and which have not entered the heart of man, all that God has prepared for those who love Him" (1 Corinthians 2:9). Paul continues in verse 10 to say that the Lord will reveal these things to us through the Spirit. In John 16:12-13, Jesus said to His disciples, "I have many more things to say to you, but you cannot bear them now. But when He, the Spirit of truth, comes, He will guide you into all truth; for He will not speak on His own initiative, but whatever He hears, He will speak; and He will disclose to you what is to come."

It is vital then that we, the church, honor and submit to the Holy Spirit, diligently study the Word of God, discover what is rightfully ours in Christ, and lead the way into this new era of awareness of spiritual sensitivity and Kingdom reality. How will we ever learn to discern the counterfeit if we are not familiar with the real thing? How will the unsaved ever embrace the truth if they only know the false?

ONE SAVIOR, ONE LORD, ONE GLORIOUS ETERNAL KING

There is one Savior, one Lord, and one glorious and eternal King – Jesus Christ the righteous! His ways are unsearchable. His glory is magnificent. His power is unparalleled. His love is unfailing. His wisdom is beyond comprehension. Oh, what a truly awesome God we serve!

My passion in writing this course is to awaken hunger in believers for all that Scripture offers in the area of God-encounters – deep intimacy with Jesus and authentic Kingdom experience in His glory. Valid spiritual experience and enhanced spiritual sensitivity are awaiting believers in this hour. May we become comfortable with biblical terms and concepts such as: third heaven, throne room, heavenly places, angels, living creatures around the throne, rainbows, glory clouds, heavenly colors and gems, spirit transport, dreams, visions, and heavenly fragrance. The Lord desires to open our spiritual eyes and ears to see, to hear and to understand things that we possibly have not even dreamt of yet in our wildest imaginations. His Kingdom is vast and magnificent, full of every good thing, and He wants us to explore and experience this realm with Him.

Introduction Notes

WORSHIP, EMPHASIS ON THE WORD, SUBMISSION TO THE HOLY SPIRIT, AND FAITH...

Extravagant worship and focus on Jesus, emphasis on the Word, submission to the Holy Spirit, and faith will be found in the following pages of this course as our basis and foundation for all spiritual Kingdom encounters.

We will definitely need to live from a heavenly perspective in these last days. There will be great turmoil and treachery in the earth, but we, the glorious church, are seated "with Him in the heavenly places in Christ Jesus" (Ephesians 2:6). We are to live our lives from a different viewpoint than those without Christ. We are to be a people who are focused on the heavenly and the divine. We are to set our affections upon Him! He is the sole object of our worship and our trust. "Therefore if you have been raised up with Christ, keep seeking the things above, where Christ is, seated at the right hand of God" (Colossians 3:1). Oh, that we would truly be such a people!

GOD ENCOUNTERS

Have you ever imagined yourself eating and drinking with God on sapphire streets, entering a glorious cloud of His Presence, gazing at the Lord high on His throne while His kingly train fills the temple, or personally encountering angels? Have you ever, in your wildest dreams, contemplated the possibilities of literally outrunning chariots, observing the armies of heaven in action, being suspended between heaven and earth by the locks of your hair like Ezekiel, or being supernaturally transported from one geographical location to another by the Spirit of God?

Could these types of divine events possibly become commonplace for us in this current era of spiritual awakening? Dare we allow the Lord, should He desire, to fill our life with God-directed and inspired supernatural occurrences as we find in the scriptural examples just mentioned? And if so, what purpose would this serve?

How could traveling in the spirit, seeing an angel, or hanging out in the throne zone enhance our worship and devotion of the King of

A Prophetic Overview

Kings in any way? How could such experiences possibly make us stronger Christians and deepen our intimacy with Jesus?

In this course, we will discover through Scripture that such encounters are not only possible in a believer's experience, should the Holy Spirit lead in that way, but that the Lord actually desires us to participate with Him in supernatural Kingdom life.

Most believers are absolutely desperate to experience the Lord and His supernatural Kingdom glory in tangible and meaningful ways. Most believers are longing to experience intimacy with Jesus, to behold His glory and to stand in His presence.

IS DESIRE FOR "GOD-EXPERIENCE" VALID?

I have found many Christians to be concerned and opposed to "experience" orientation. Although I agree that we are to be careful not to worship "experience," I would like to gently and respectfully challenge their concern.

Successful and meaningful relationships are based on a choice to love as well as to experience that love. If you were to take the experience dimension out of a relationship, you would more than likely be left with a cold and empty association and not a relationship at all.

Here is an example:

Can you imagine standing at the altar waiting to make a life-commitment to your bride who is walking down the aisle toward you, all decked out in her elaborate bridal apparel – looking more ravishing than you have ever seen her? Your heart is pounding. You are *experiencing* intense waves of passionate love and anticipation that are washing over your affections for her. She finally makes her way to the front, standing beside you in all of her bridal radiance. You begin to make your vows. She looks at you with sincerity during this moment of sealing a lifelong covenant and says tenderly and with conviction, "I vow to be your wife, to be faithful to you, to submit to you ... but don't expect to *experience* my love ... I'm not into experience ... I don't want our marriage to be based on experience ... oh, no ... and I don't expect to *experience* your love either ... I will simply believe that you love me, but I will not expect nor will I pursue *experience* in our relationship."

Oh my, what a disappointment to the bridegroom. Perhaps he will change his mind right there at the altar. Why? Because, experience has everything to do with relationship. It is impossible to enjoy a rich and meaningful relationship without experience. Experience is absolutely essential. Of course the balance to this is based on an unshakable, quality decision to commit to the relationship.

You will not become acquainted with the qualities of a person simply by reading a biography about them. You will really come to know them, however, by spending time with them: communicating, listening, and interacting. This is how it works in our walk with the Lord, too. He desires us to know Him intimately. He desires us to experience His love, His kindness, and His truth. He would be so disappointed if we said, "Reading the Bible is all I need. I can find everything I need to know about You, Lord, through Your Word. It doesn't matter to me if I experience Your love or not." This would break His heart. He longs to experience relationship with us. When He was suffering on the cross, He had an expectation. He endured the cross for the joy set before Him. Experiencing an eternal love relationship with you was that joy.

The Lord Desires Us to Experience His Kingdom

Not only are we invited to experience the Lord Himself, He also desires us to experience His Kingdom. I am a Canadian and have lived most of my life in North American culture. I am Canadian because I have paperwork to prove that I was born in Canada. It is the daily experiences in my nation and culture, however, that have actually caused me to be Canadian in lifestyle, appearance and personality. I have for years experienced Canadian culture and therefore act and function as a Canadian. This North American flair did not come from studying the Canadian Constitution; it came through daily experience in the culture. The laws of our land definitely form and shape the perimeters of acceptable activity within our nation, but it is actually experience within that framework that gives my fellow Canadians the noted Canadian personality.

A Prophetic Overview

I have traveled into many nations and have noticed that there are distinct characteristics between cultures and peoples. I am able, in most cases, to tell the difference between an American and a Canadian, or between someone from Germany and someone from Holland, even though the nations that I have just mentioned are right next to each other. I can usually tell the difference between an Afro-American with Nigerian heritage and a Nigerian who was born and raised in Africa. Experience and life in their culture and environment has made the distinction.

It is the same for us as children of God. The Lord desires us to fully experience His Kingdom. As we do so, we will begin to take on the profile of a Kingdom citizen. Our citizenship in this glorious eternal dominion is secured once we accept Jesus Christ as our Savior. As a Kingdom child there are many blessings and benefits that have been granted us. In this domain, we will find the Sovereign Lord governing over the universe; we will become acquainted with the glory of His presence and His majesty. We are invited to behold Him and His wonderful love. There is so much to discover. There is a place called heaven within this Kingdom. There are angels, chariots, fiery ones around the throne, a crystal sea, a river of life, the tree of life, the great cloud of witnesses, golden streets, and oh, so much more! The Word of God is full of information and revelation regarding the Kingdom of God, and we have been invited to discover and to partake.

"Do not be afraid, little flock, for your Father has chosen gladly to give you the kingdom."   —Luke 12:32

"But seek first His kingdom and His righteousness, and all these things will be added to you."   —Matthew 6:33

Days of Tumult and Tension

Throughout the Scriptures we find that the times when most of the supernatural empowerments of God were witnessed were during days of great tumult and tension. During Bible times when peace was in the land, you do not find too much written in the Scriptures regarding God's mighty works. Moses lived in very oppressed days and yet he experienced so many awesome acts in the presence of the Lord.

Elijah, Elisha, Daniel, David, Jeremiah, Ezekiel, and Isaiah as well as Christ's disciples and the believers in the book of Acts also witnessed and experienced many supernatural and divine occurrences. A great deal of space is given in the Scripture to all that the Lord did during these times of pressure and trials. During seasons of peace you might find a one-liner that goes something like this: "So-and-so reigned for so many years and there was peace in the land."

We are headed into some treacherous days – days of great tumult and tension. God is going to prepare us for what is ahead. He will teach us how to experience Him, His Kingdom and His power in greater ways. Simply attending a service or a conference, or engaging in a church program, will no longer get us through the days ahead. We will need to know Him and experience Him like never before. We will definitely need to learn to walk and war as true Kingdom children, living in true Kingdom consecration, power and grace.

The Bible is full of accounts of God-encounters. If you were to remove all the records of experience out of the Bible, leaving only the doctrine, there would be very little left.

Experience orientation is valid if it has a place of right priority within our heart. Experience, for the sake of experience, however, has no eternal value at all, and the idolatry of it could possibly lead to great deception. Experience in knowing Him, His Kingdom and His righteousness, however, is our upward call in Christ Jesus.

> But whatever things were gain to me, those things I have counted as loss for the sake of Christ.
>
> **That I may know Him**, and the power of His resurrection and the fellowship of His sufferings, being conformed to His death.
>
> Brethren, I do not regard myself as having laid hold of it yet; but one thing I do: forgetting what lies behind and reaching forward to what lies ahead, I press on toward the goal for the prize of the upward call of God in Christ Jesus.
> —Philippians 3:7,10,13-14

Lesson One

The Cross and the Covenant

1 John 3:1; 4:16-19; Romans 8:32-39; 1 Corinthians 13

A. The Cross and Our Eternal Covenant

An understanding of the work of the Cross and the eternal covenant that the Father cut with the Son is an essential foundation for experiencing heavenly glory.

1. God desired relationship with man. He longed to share His love and His goodness with His own children, and that is why He created mankind.

2. He knew man would sin against Him even before He created man. He knows all things. God is omniscient.

3. God chose to put His love to a remarkable test: the Cross – the testing place of love. He chose the Cross to be the place where the blood covenant would be cut.

4. Because man sinned, God could not have fellowship with him, but man could not restore himself.

Lesson One Notes

5. God chose to restore mankind through an unbreakable eternal covenant. God Himself would set the terms. God Himself would fulfill the terms. This covenant would culminate with the shedding of blood and a giving of His own life for man at the Cross.

6. God's motive for reconciling man to Himself through the Cross of the covenant was unconditional love.

B. Covenant

1. Definition of Covenant

    a. A binding agreement between two parties

    b. "Where the blood flows" (cutting covenant – blood covenant), a cut in the flesh (i.e., marriage covenant)

    c. Common in ancient civilizations between tribes

    d. Exchanges:

       1. Vows – conditions of the covenant are set between the representatives of the two parties

       2. Blood – covenant cut and the mingling of blood

       3. Names

       4. Clothing

       5. Weapons (enemies also)

       6. Wealth

       7. Covenant meal

2. Examples of covenants within the Bible

    a. Abraham and Abimelech —Genesis 21:22-34

    b. Jonathan and David —1 Samuel 18:3; 20:8; 23:18

    c. Israel and the Amorites —1 Samuel 7:14

Lesson One Notes

3. God makes covenant with His people

   a. With Abraham (the covenant of faith)   —Genesis 17:7-19

   b. With Moses (the covenant of the law)   —Exodus 24:7-8

   c. A new and better covenant   —Hebrews 8

C. Our Eternal Unbreakable Covenant
—Hebrews 8–13

1. Conditions of the Covenant

   a. God would give eternal life to man if the terms were fulfilled.

   b. Jesus, as man's representative, had to fulfill all the law and the prophets.

   c. Jesus, as man's representative, had to pay fair punishment (death) for man's sins.

   d. Man had to believe in Christ in order to enter into covenant.

2. Jesus – the Son of God (Jesus represented God in covenant)

   a. In Him all the fullness of Deity dwells in bodily form. —Colossians 2:9

   b. God was in Christ reconciling the world to Himself. —2 Corinthians 5:19

   c. He remitted the sins of all.   —Luke 23:34

3. Jesus – the Son of Man (incarnated through the virgin birth and represented man in covenant)

   a. The Son of Man has come to save that which was lost. —Matthew 18:11

   b. Jesus – the last Adam   —1 Corinthians 15:45

   c. As a man, on behalf of mankind, Jesus fulfilled all the terms

Lesson One Notes

of the covenant that needed to be fulfilled by man:

1. All the law and the prophets —Matthew 5:17
2. All righteousness —Matthew 3:15
3. Entered into repentance for all through His baptism —Matthew 3:13-17
4. Identified with man's sin —2 Corinthians 5:21
5. Identified with man's poverty —2 Corinthians 8:9
6. Entered into death for all —Romans 5:6-8
7. Paid the penalty for all —Isaiah 53
8. Was raised for all —Romans 6:3-9
9. The blood was shed – the Cross

4. The Exchange
   a. Names – "In My name" —Mark 16:15-20; John 14:13-14
   b. Clothing (His armor) —Ephesians 6:13-17
   c. Weapons (strength, might, victories) —2 Corinthians 10:3-5
   d. Wealth —2 Corinthians 8:9; Philippians 4:19
   e. Covenant meal —1 Corinthians 11:23-26

5. The Power of the Blood of the Covenant —Hebrews 9:20
   a. Gives life —John 6:53-54
   b. Purchases our lives for God —Acts 20:28
   c. Propitiation —Romans 3:25
   d. Justification —Romans 5:9
   e. Communion with God —1 Corinthians 10:16
   f. Redemption —Ephesians 1:7; Revelation 5:9; Colossians 1:14

g. Forgiveness —Ephesians 1:7

h. Brought near to God —Ephesians 2:13

i. Gives peace —Colossians 1:20

j. Cleanses conscience —Hebrews 9:14

k. Forgiveness of sins —Hebrews 9:22

l. Entrance into the holy place —Hebrews 10:19

m. Deliverance from the judgment and wrath of God —Hebrews 11:28

n. Cleanses from sin —1 John 1:7; Revelation 1:5, 7:14

o. Resurrection power —Hebrews 13:20

p. Sanctifies —Hebrews 13:12

q. Overcoming power —Revelation 12:11

r. Bears witness —1 John 5:8

6. The Outcome

a. God's love was perfectly proven and could never be questioned.

b. Man would never be separated from the love of God. —Romans 8:35-39

c. Man was offered an eternally secure relationship with God through believing in the finished work of Christ on the cross. "By grace you have been saved through faith." —Ephesians 2:8

d. The Father's desire for children was fulfilled through those who would believe in Christ. —John 1:12

e. Redeemed man was invited to be a partaker in the heavenly glory and was invited to freely access the throne of grace through the blood of the covenant —Hebrews 4:16; 10:19–22 (very important Scriptures)

Lesson One Notes

Lesson One Notes

D. Jesus Christ – To Be Exalted and Worshipped

The rule of Jesus is over all – He is fully God and fully Man.

1. Jesus, our Almighty God; Eternal Father   —Isaiah 9:6; Revelation 1:7-8

2. Jesus, our Savior (Jesus = "Jehovah is Salvation")   —Matthew 1:21

3. Jesus, our Righteousness   —Jeremiah 23:6; Romans 3:10-26

4. Jesus, our Intercessor, our Mediator
   —Hebrews 7:25; 1 Timothy 2:5

   Intercessor – one who stands between two parties; a mediator; one who interposes between two parties and is a friend to both

5. Jesus, our Surety   —Hebrews 7:22 (NKJV)

   Surety – a person who takes responsibility for another; one who accepts liabilities for another's debts, defaults of obligations, etc.; a guarantee

6. Jesus, our Captain   —Joshua 5:13-15; Revelation 19:11-16

7. Jesus, our Shepherd and Guide   —Psalm 23

8. Jesus, our Healer and Deliverer   —1 Peter 2:24; 2 Timothy 4:18

9. Jesus, our Lord and King   —Revelation 19:16; 1 Timothy 1:17

10. Jesus, our Friend   —Matthew 11:19

11. Jesus, our Way, Truth, Life   —John 14:6

12. Jesus, our Bridegroom   —Revelation 19:7

E. Conclusion

Let this mind be in you which was also in Christ Jesus, who, being in the form of God, did not consider it robbery to be equal with God, but made Himself of no reputation, taking the form of a bondservant, and coming in the likeness of men.

And being found in appearance as a man, He humbled Himself and became obedient to the point of death, even the death of the cross.

Therefore God also has highly exalted Him and given Him the name which is above every name, that at the name of Jesus every knee should bow, of those in heaven, and of those on earth, and of those under the earth, and that every tongue should confess that Jesus Christ is Lord, to the glory of God the Father.

—Philippians 2:5-11 (NKJV)

LESSON TWO

NEW CREATION REALITIES

Notes

A. THE NEW CREATION —2 CORINTHIANS 5:17

1. Man is spirit, he has a soul and he lives in a body.
   —1 Thessalonians 5:23

    a. Creation of man   —Genesis 2:7

2. The spirit – relates to the spirit realm

    a. A believer receives a "new spirit" and the Holy Spirit dwells within the spirit man of a born-again Christian.
       —Ezekiel 36:26-27; John 3:6

    b. The spirit is "in Christ" when a person is born-again.
       —Galatians 5:6; 2 Corinthians 5:17

    c. The "spirit man" of a born-again Christian is made in the very image and likeness of Christ.   —1 Corinthians 6:17; Ephesians 4:24; Colossians 3:10

    d. The born-again spirit man does not sin.   —1 John 3:9

    e. The spirit under the leading and dominion of the Holy Spirit is to rule over the soul and body.   —Galatians 5:16

Lesson Two Notes

    f. The born-again spirit is acquainted with the divine, heavenly realm. —Revelation 1:10-20; 21:10

    g. All that pertains to life and godliness is already within the born-again spirit. —2 Peter 1:2-4

    h. All the spiritual blessings in the heavenly places in Christ are already within the born-again spirit. —Ephesians 1:3

3. The soul (mind, will, emotions) – relates to the intellectual, emotional and relational realm.

    a. The soul's faculty of intellect or mind —Psalm 139:14; Proverbs 2:10; 19:2

    b. The soul's faculty of emotion —Song of Songs 1:7; Luke 1:46; 2 Samuel 5:8; Psalm 107:18; Zechariah 11:8

    c. The soul's faculty of volition —Psalm 27:12; 41:2; Job 6:7 (AMP)

    d. The soul is who we are. It is the seat of our personality. It makes our choices, determines our likes, our dislikes, our values. Oftentimes in Scripture an individual is referred to as "a soul." —1 Peter 3:20; Acts 27:37; Romans 2:9

    e. The soul makes a decision on whether it will obey the body and its lusts or the spirit and the nature of Christ. The soul makes the decision. If the soul does not choose to walk in the born-again spirit directed by the Holy Spirit, then it will walk in the flesh. There is no neutrality.

    f. The mind is to be renewed through choosing to walk in the born-again spirit. —Ephesians 4:23-24

    g. If the soul chooses to walk in the Spirit, the fruit of the Spirit will be evident and the nature of Christ will be made manifest. —Galatians 5:22-25; Ephesians 4:24

4. The body – relates to the physical and earthly realm.

    a. The body was originally made from the dust of the earth and therefore relates to the earthly realm or the worldly realm —Genesis 2:7

Lesson Two Notes

    b. The body's purpose in the Kingdom is to radiate and manifest the glory of the Lord and to fulfill Christ's purposes.   —Isaiah 60:1-3; Exodus 34:29; Matthew 17:2

    c. We are to submit our body and its members to righteousness.   —Romans 6:19

5. The flesh; the carnal nature, the "old self" – relates to the unredeemed nature of man; the part of the body and soul that is set against the Spirit; the self-rule part of man.   —Ephesians 4:22; Colossians 3:9; Romans 8:7

    a. Unrighteousness

    b. Self-righteousness

    c. "That which is born of flesh is flesh."   —John 3:6

    d. The sin of the flesh   —Romans 7:23

    e. Must be reckoned **dead** through the finished work of the cross   —Galatians 2:20

B. THE CRUCIFIED LIFE

1. I have been crucified with Christ – not, "I hope to be," or "I will try to be."   —Galatians 2:20; Romans 6:6

2. I do not crucify myself. Christ already died for me on the cross.

3. By faith, I appropriate this death to my flesh (carnal nature), my old self.   —Romans 6:11-13

4. I am dead and my life is hidden with Christ in God. —Colossians 3:3

5. Death before resurrection   —Philippians 3:10-11

6. The Holy Spirit helps us to appropriate the power of the Cross to our flesh and reckon it dead.

Lesson Two Notes

C. The Christ-Life

1. Jesus is the resurrection and the life.   —John 11:25

    a. We are called to live by Christ's life.   —Romans 6:4-11

    b. The Christ-life that we live in the flesh, we live by faith.
       —Galatians 2:20

    c. The Holy Spirit helps us to live in our new Christ-life.

D. Kingdom Children   —Hebrews 12:28

1. A kingdom is a place or territory where a king has rule.

2. As covenant children and new creations in Christ, we belong to God's Kingdom, ruled by Christ.

3. As covenant kingdom children, we have been given all things to enjoy.

E. Who We Are As Covenant Children
(non-exhaustive)

1. The righteousness of God in Christ   —2 Corinthians 5:21

2. Fellow heirs with Jesus   —Galatians 4:7, Romans 8:16-17

3. Ambassadors for Christ   —2 Corinthians 5:20

4. Children of God   —John 1:12

5. The bride of Christ   —Revelation 19:7

6. The glorious church   —Ephesians 5:25-27 (NKJV)

7. The light of the world   —Matthew 5:14

8. The salt of the earth   —Matthew 5:13

9. The temple of the living God   —2 Corinthians 6:16

10. More than conquerors   —Romans 8:37 (NKJV)

11. The redeemed of the Lord —Revelation 5:9 (NKJV)

12. Overcomers —Revelation 12:11

F. WHAT WE HAVE AS COVENANT CHILDREN
(NON-EXHAUSTIVE)

1. Forgiveness —1 John 1:9

2. Freedom —Galatians 5:1

3. Grace —John 1:16

4. Truth —John 14:6

5. Health and healing —Isaiah 53:5; 1 Peter 2:24

6. Abundant life —John 10:10

7. The fruit of the Spirit —Galatians 5:22-23

8. The gifts of the Spirit —1 Corinthians 12:7-11

9. Boldness to come to the throne of grace —Hebrews 4:16 (NKJV)

10. Love —1 John 3:1

11. The Holy Spirit —John 14:16-17, 26

12. Eternal Life —John 3:16

13. Power over the enemy —Luke 10:19

14. Righteousness —Romans 3:21-24

15. Favor —Psalm 5:12

16. Every spiritual blessing in the heavenly places —Ephesians 1:3

17. Triumph in every circumstance —2 Corinthians 2:14

18. Wisdom —James 1:5

19. Precious and magnificent promises —2 Peter 1:2-4

20. Mercy —1 Peter 2:10

Lesson Two Notes

Lesson Two Notes

21. Financial provision —Philippians 4:19
22. Peace —John 14:27

LESSON THREE

THE PERSON OF THE HOLY SPIRIT

A. WHO IS THE HOLY SPIRIT?

1. He is a *person* and not a mere influence or power

2. He is referred to as part of the Godhead   —Matthew 28:19

3. He is the Promise of the Father   —Acts 1:4-5; 2:33

4. He is referred to as "Lord"   —2 Corinthians 3:18

5. He is referred to as "the seven Spirits of God before the throne"   —Revelation 4:5; Isaiah 11:2

6. He is a gift to us   —Acts 2:38

7. He comes from heaven   —1 Peter 1:12

8. He is the Spirit of the Godhead   —Romans 8:9,14

   (more teaching to discuss the Spirit, Soul and Body of the Godhead)

Lesson Three Notes

B. Titles for the Holy Spirit

(The word "spirit" found in the references below comes from the Greek word *pneuma* which refers to "the Holy Spirit, the Spirit of God, the Spirit of Christ, spirit." In the following references, we believe the context indicates God's Spirit.)

1. Spirit of God —Matthew 3:16; 12:28; Romans 8:9,14-15; 1 Corinthians 2:11-12,14; 3:16; 6:11; 12:3; Ephesians 4:30; 1 Peter 4:14; 1 John 4:2

2. Spirit of life —Romans 8:2; Revelation 11:11

3. Spirit of truth —John 15:26; 16:13; 1 John 4:6

4. Spirit of glory —1 Peter 4:14

5. Spirit of Christ —1 Peter 1:11

6. Spirit of grace —Hebrews 10:29

7. Spirit of wisdom —Ephesians 1:17

8. Spirit of revelation —Ephesians 1:17

9. Spirit of promise —Ephesians 1:13

10. Holy Spirit —Ephesians 1:13; Acts 1:8; 1 Corinthians 12:3

11. Spirit of the Son —Galatians 4:6

12. Spirit of the Lord —2 Corinthians 3:17-18; Acts 8:39; Luke 4:18; Acts 5:9

13. Spirit of the living God —2 Corinthians 3:3

14. Spirit of holiness —Romans 1:4

15. Spirit of the Father —Matthew 10:20

16. Comforter —John 15:26

C. 70 Functions of the Holy Spirit
(Found in the New Testament)

1. Leads/Directs —Matthew 4:1; Mark 1:12; Luke 2:27; 4:1; Romans 8:14; Acts 8:29

2. Speaks (in, to and through) —Matthew 10:20; Acts 1:16; 2:4; 13:2; 28:25; Hebrews 3:7

3. Casts out demons —Matthew 12:28

4. Releases power —Luke 4:14

5. Anointing —Luke 4:18; Acts 10:38

6. Comes upon/falls on —Matthew 3:16; Mark 1:10; Luke 2:25; 3:22; 4:18; John 1:32-33; Acts 10:44; 11:15

7. Baptized/filled with —Matthew 3:11; Mark 1:8; Luke 1:15, 41, 67; 3:16; 4:1; John 1:33; Acts 1:4-5; 2:4; 4:8, 31; 6:3,5; 7:55; 10:47; 11:24; 13:9, 52; 1 Corinthians 12:13

8. Gives new birth —John 3:5,8

9. Leads into worship —John 4:23

10. Flows like a river from the spirit man —John 7:38, 39

11. Ministers truth —John 14:17; 15:26; 16:13

12. Dwells in —John 14:17; Romans 8:9,11; 1 Corinthians 3:16

13. Comfort, health, and strength —John 15:26; Acts 9:31

14. He proceeds from the Father —John 15:26

15. Shows us things to come —John 16:13

16. Gives the gift of tongues —Acts 2:4

17. Releases prophecy, dreams, vision —Acts 2:17-18; 11:28

18. Transports —Acts 8:39

Lesson Three Notes

Lesson Three Notes

19. Brings direction, guidance —Mark 12:36; 13:11; Acts 10:19; 11:12; 21:11; 1 Timothy 4:1

20. Holiness —Romans 1:4

21. Spirit of Life, gives Life (Zoe) —Romans 8:1,10

22. Invites us to walk with Him —Romans 8:4-5

23. Groans, prayer, intercession —Romans 8:26-27

24. Sword (the rhema) —Ephesians 6:17

25. Produces fruit —Galatians 5:22-23; Ephesians 5:9

26. Helps us in weakness —Romans 8:26

27. Bears witness —Acts 5:32; 15:28; 20:23; Romans 8:15-16; Hebrews 10:15; 1 John 4:13; 5:6-8

28. Spirit of adoption —Romans 8:15

29. Gives power to mortify the deeds of flesh —Romans 8:13

30. Ministers power – signs, wonders, preaching —Acts 1:8; 1 Corinthians 2:4

31. Ministers love —Romans 15:30

32. Searches deep things of God —1 Corinthians 2:10

33. Quickens the mortal body —Romans 8:13

34. Brings revelation —Luke 2:25; 1 Corinthians 2:10-12; Ephesians 1:17-19; 3:5

35. Reveals to us what has been given by God —1 Corinthians 2:12

36. Washes, sanctifies, purifies, justifies —Romans 15:16; 1 Corinthians 6:11; 2 Thessalonians 2:13; 1 Timothy 3:16; 1 Peter 1:2, 22

37. Has gifts —1 Corinthians 12:4-11; Hebrews 2:4

38. Seals us —2 Corinthians 1:22; Ephesians 4:30

The Person of the Holy Spirit

Lesson Three Notes

39. Liberty   —2 Corinthians 3:17

40. Changes us into the image of Christ   —2 Corinthians 3:18

41. Promise of the blessing of Abraham   —Galatians 3:14

42. Releases a cry to the Father   —Galatians 4:6

43. Gives access unto the Father   —Ephesians 2:18

44. Builds us together for a habitation for God   —Ephesians 2:22

45. Strengthens us with might   —Ephesians 3:16

46. Unity   —Ephesians 4:3-4

47. Wine   —Ephesians 5:18

48. Supplies   —Philippians 1:19

49. Fellowship   —2 Corinthians 13:14; Philippians 2:1

50. Grace   —Hebrews 10:29

51. Glory   —1 Peter 4:14

52. Speaks to the churches   —Revelation 2:11, 17, 29; 3:6, 13, 22

53. Calls for the Bridegroom   —Revelation 22:17

54. Conception of anointings and God's purposes   —Matthew 1:18, 20; Luke 1:35

55. Teaches   —Luke 12:12; John 14:26; 1 Corinthians 2:13; 1 John 2:27

56. Gives commandments   —Acts 1:2

57. Power to be a witness (martyr)   —Acts 1:8

58. Boldness   —Acts 4:31

59. Gives sight   —Acts 9:17

60. Commissions   —Acts 13:4

Lesson Three Notes

61. Restrains   —Acts 16:6
62. Appoints ministries/gives authority   —Acts 20:28
63. Releases love   —Romans 5:5
64. Righteousness, peace and joy   —Romans 14:17; 15:13; 1 Thessalonians 1:6
65. Confession of Christ's Lordship   —1 Corinthians 12:3
66. Brings the Gospel   —1 Thessalonians 1:5-6
67. Keeping power– 2 Timothy 1:14
68. Brings renewal – Titus 3:5
69. Moves on believers   —2 Peter 1:21
70. Convicts the world   —John 16:8

D. THE BELIEVER AND THE HOLY SPIRIT

1. We are His temple   —1 Corinthians 6:19
2. We are partakers of   —Hebrews 6:4
3. We are to receive Him by
   a. laying on of hands   —Acts 8:17; 19:2-6
   b. breath   —John 20:22
   c. being prayed for   —Acts 8:15
   d. speaking   —Acts 10:44-45; 11:15-16
4. We are not to:
   a. tempt   —Acts 5:9
   b. lie to   —Acts 5:3
   c. resist   —Acts 7:51; Romans 8:9-26
   d. grieve   —Ephesians 4:30

e. quench   —1 Thessalonians 5:19

f. blaspheme   —Mark 3:28-29

   blaspheme = slander; speech injurous to divine majesty

5. We are to go and baptize in His name   —Matthew 28:19

6. We are to move in His gifts   —1 Corinthians 12, 14

7. We are to pray in the Holy Spirit   —Jude 1:20

8. We are to fellowship with Him   —2 Corinthians 13:14

E. Communion with the Holy Spirit

"The grace of our Lord Jesus Christ, and the love of God, and the communion of the Holy Spirit be with you all."   —2 Corinthians 13:14

(some of this outline comes from the book, Good Morning Holy Spirit, by Benny Hinn)

Communion means:

1. Presence. God the Father's desire for you is that the sweet presence of the Holy Spirit will be with you.

2. Fellowship. You do not need to pray to the Holy Spirit; you simply fellowship with Him.

3. Sharing together. You pour out your heart and He pours out His. You share your joy and He shares His. "It seemed good to the Holy Spirit, and to us," wrote the apostles to the believers in Antioch   —Acts 15:28

4. Participation with. The Holy Spirit becomes your partner. The Scripture, filled with phrases like "working with them" and "the Spirit and us," makes it clear that the work of the Spirit is in participation with you.

5. Intimacy. You'll never experience a deep love with Christ until you know it with the Holy Spirit who brings that intimacy.

Lesson Three Notes

There is no other way. You can't love God without the Holy Spirit. God has "poured out" His love into our hearts "through the Holy Spirit who was given to us."   —Romans 5:5

6. Friendship. The Spirit longs to be your closest friend, someone with whom you can share the deepest secrets of your heart.

7. Comradeship. A comrade is a friend in battle. In Greek the word means "commander." He's like a captain, a ruler, or a boss – but a loving, friendly one. Just as He instructed the apostles where they should go and where they shouldn't, He must be allowed to rule your personal affairs.

F. Developing a Relationship with the Holy Spirit

"The grace of our Lord Jesus Christ, and the love of God, and the fellowship of the Holy Spirit be with you all."   —2 Corinthians 13:14

1. Acknowledge Him – His presence, gifts, nature, functions

2. Thank Him for coming to you

3. Invite Him to take control of your life and decisions

4. Invite Him to lead you and to counsel you – remember, He authored the Scriptures   —2 Peter 1:20-21

5. Fellowship (dialogue) with Him as you would with a friend

6. Journal

7. Look for Him and His activities throughout your day

8. Be available to Him should He desire to use you to release His manifested presence

9. Be ready to obey Him

10. Repent when you sense that you have grieved Him

11. Enjoy Him

12. Rest in His love

G. Developing a Prayer Time with the Holy Spirit

(some of this outline comes from the book, *Good Morning Holy Spirit*, by Benny Hinn)

Seven Steps to Prayer:

1. Confession: Begin by acknowledging who God is. Declare the power of the Almighty. Confess what is true about God. Declare His names, etc.

2. Supplication: Supplication means to request favor. You have favor because of the grace that God showed to you through Christ. Begin to make request for favors. Ask Him to bestow wisdom and counsel and might upon you. Invite Him to communion with you. The Holy Spirit can lead you to bring your supplications before the Father. He can reveal to you what you have received through Christ. These are the things that you can freely ask the Father for.

3. Adoration: This should be a time of beauty and worship as you love Jesus and adore Him. You may begin with the words, "Jesus, I love You," or "Jesus, You are so good, so lovely, so kind." As you exalt Jesus, you will often begin to feel the Holy Spirit's presence.

4. Intimacy: Adoration will lead you into deep levels of interaction with the Lord. Yield your heart to Him as you worship and adore Him. Share your love and allow Him to share His with you.

5. Intercession: When you invite the Holy Spirit to help you pray, He will share His heart with you in regards to others. Often in the place of intimacy He will begin to share His desires and His plans, and He will bring the names and faces of people before you so you can pray for them. You will know how to pray for others because you will be in heart-to-heart communication.

Lesson Three Notes

Lesson Three Notes

6. Thanksgiving: Give thanks to the Father, the Son, and the Holy Spirit.

7. Praise: Praise Him for His goodness, His power, His love. Exalt the name of Jesus. Praise Him with your whole heart.

Lesson Four

Faith: The Connector to Heavenly Glory

Faith is the "connector" which secures the covenant blessings that were wrought through Christ's finished work on the cross, bringing them into our experiential realm. It is very important that we understand how to release our faith in order to experience the realms of heavenly glory.

A. Faith: the Foundation for all Spiritual Experience

1. We cannot please God without it —Hebrews 11:6

2. Every man has a measure of faith —Romans 12:3

3. It is the victory that overcomes the world —1 John 5:4

4. It is the substance and evidence of spiritual things —Hebrews 11:1

5. Faith creates things that are not —Romans 4:16-25

6. Faith is a force from God, given as a gift —Mark 11:2-3; Ephesians 2:8-10

Lesson Four Notes

B. Our Salvation is Based on Faith Alone

1. Ephesians 2:8
2. Hebrews 11:6

C. Blessings and Promises Are Appropriated by Faith

1. Ephesians 1:3
2. 2 Peter 1:2-4
3. Romans 1:17
4. Matthew 6:10

D. Steps to Releasing Faith

1. Faith hears   —Romans 10:17

    a. Rhema vs. logos

    b. True faith is always birthed and led by the Holy Spirit and is not "presumption."

    c. Positioning yourself to hear – intimacy

2. Faith sees   —Genesis 13:14-15; Habakkuk 2:1-3

    God's vision or ??

3. Faith speaks   —Romans 10:8-10

    a. The power of the tongue   —James 3:1-12

    b. Your words release faith   —2 Corinthians 4:13

    c. Out of the abundance of the heart   —Matthew 12:34 (NKJV)

4. Faith rejoices   —Philippians 4:6

5. Faith is thankful   —1 Thessalonians 5:6-18

Faith: The Connector to Heavenly Glory

      a. The consequence of murmuring/complaining

6. Faith acts —James 2:14-26

    a. Be a doer of the Word —James 1:22

7. Faith persists and endures —Galatians 6:9

    a. P.U.S.H. (Pray until something happens) —Matthew 17:20

    b. Abraham hoped against hope —Romans 4:16-18

    c. The watchmen who take no rest —Isaiah 62:6-7

    d. O.T. believers who endured in faith —Hebrews 11:13

    e. Parable of the unjust judge —Luke 18:1-8

    f. Jacob persisted and prevailed —Genesis 32:26-29

8. Faith fights —1 Timothy 6:12

9. Faith rests —Hebrews 4:1-12

10. Faith receives —Mark 11:24

    a. When you pray.

Lesson Four Notes

Notes

LESSON FIVE

THE WORD OF GOD: OUR BASIS FOR EXPERIENCE

"Thy word is a lamp unto my feet and a light unto my path."
—Psalm 119:105

All spiritual experience must be rooted and grounded on the foundation and the plumb line of the Word of God. We are to be lovers of His Word and those who will cleave to it.

Attributes of the Word of God:

1. Eternal in the heavens —Matthew 24:35

2. Is truth —John 17:17

3. Shall not return void —Isaiah 55:11 (NKJV)

4. Frames the will of God —Hebrews 11:3 (NKJV)

5. Dispatches angels —Psalm 103:20

6. Brings light into darkness —Psalm 119:130

7. Is a lamp to our feet and a light to our path —Psalm 119:105

8. Secures blessings —Ephesians 1:3; 2 Peter 1:2-4

Lesson Five Notes

9. The Word is seed —Mark 4
10. Weapon of warfare —2 Corinthians 10:3-5; Ephesians 6
11. Pulls down mindsets —2 Corinthians 10:3-5
12. Creates —Romans 4:17
13. Sanctifies —John 17:17
14. Strengthens the spirit man —Ephesians 3:16
15. Ensures answers to prayer —John 15:7
16. Separates soul from spirit —Hebrews 4:12

LESSON SIX

THE REWARDS OF HOLINESS

A. WHAT IS HOLINESS?

1. To be holy means to be set apart for God and His purposes. Once something or someone is declared holy, it is no longer to be used for mundane purposes. *Holiness* means "set-apartness," "sacredness." It includes moral purity and purification.

2. Anything that is set apart as holy belongs to God and is for His purposes.

3. Holiness is not what you do but it is who you are.

4. Holiness is not a set of rules that are obeyed.

5. Holiness is a spirit – part of God's spiritual nature.

   "And declared to be the Son of God with power, according to the spirit of holiness, by the resurrection from the dead."
   —Romans 1:4

Lesson Six Notes

B. How Do We Become Holy?

1. It is God Himself who makes us holy – sets us apart for Himself – in spirit, soul and body.

   "And the very God of peace sanctify you wholly; and I pray God your whole spirit and soul and body be preserved blameless unto the coming of our Lord Jesus Christ. Faithful is he that calls you, who also will do it."
   —1 Thessalonians 5:23-24 (KJV)

2. Jesus Christ is our holiness and sanctifies us.

   "But of Him are you in Christ Jesus, who of God is made unto us wisdom, and righteousness, and sanctification, and redemption."   —1 Corinthians 1:30 (KJV)

   "For both He who sanctifies and those who are sanctified are all from one Father; for which reason He is not ashamed to call them brethren."   —Hebrews 2:11

   Wherefore Jesus also, that he might sanctify the people with his own blood, suffered without the gate.   —Hebrews 13:12 (KJV)

3. The Holy Spirit makes us holy (sanctifies).

   "Such were some of you; but you were washed, but you were sanctified, but you were justified in the name of the Lord Jesus Christ and in the Spirit of our God."   —1 Corinthians 6:11

   (Note: The Holy Spirit is called the *Holy* Spirit and not "the worldly spirit" or "the unclean spirit" or "the lustful spirit."

4. The Word sanctifies.

   "Sanctify them in the truth; Your word is truth.... For their sakes I sanctify Myself, that they themselves also may be sanctified in truth."   —John 17:17,19

   So that He might sanctify her, having cleansed her by the washing of water with the word."   —Ephesians 5:26

The Rewards of Holiness

Lesson Six Notes

5. We sanctify ourselves.

    "But sanctify Christ as Lord in your hearts." —1 Peter 3:15

    "But like the Holy One who called you, be holy yourselves also in all your behavior; because it is written, 'You shall be holy, for I am holy.'" —1 Peter 1:15-16

6. At our rebirth, our spirit was made holy. We were saved and given a new life that is in the image of Christ.

    "Therefore if anyone is in Christ, he is a new creature; the old things passed away; behold, new things have come." —2 Corinthians 5:17

7. Our soul and body are to submit to the gift of this new life that has been created in holiness. By putting on this "new man," the soul and body will also manifest holiness.

    "And put on the new self, which in the likeness of God has been created in righteousness and holiness of the truth." —Ephesians 4:24

8. Holiness is chosen by our will out of relationship with God. Because we love Him and enjoy fellowship with Him, as "set apart ones" we learn to love what He loves and hate what He hates. Remember: holiness is not a set of rules that are obeyed. When we understand and walk in our "set-apartness" by faith and in a love relationship, we will do the things that we see our Father do. We will love and embrace the very things He loves. We will hate the things that He dislikes. We will share His heart and thus manifest His holiness in our spirit, soul and body.

    The spirit of holiness is the heart of holiness. In other words, the source of holiness is not in what we do but it is found in the heart behind what we do.

    "God's pleasure or displeasure is not founded upon the principle of good and evil. Rather, God traces the source of all things. An action may be quite correct, yet God inquires, 'what is its origin'?" —*The Spiritual Man*, Watchman Nee

Lesson Six Notes

9. The Holy Spirit is our holiness mentor. We recognize our complete dependency on Him to lead and guide us. He leads us in God's ways and reveals God's heart to us.

C. WHAT DOES GOD LOVE AND WHAT DOES HE HATE?

"You have loved righteousness and hated wickedness; Therefore God, Your God, has anointed You with the oil of joy above Your fellows."   —Psalm 45:7

(Note: It is good for each believer to engage in his/her own search as he or she reaches out to know Him, inviting the Holy Spirit to reveal God's heart. Ask the Lord questions – questions like: "Why do You like or not like this?" and "Why is this important to You?" The following is a list of only a few things that the Scripture teaches us regarding what the Lord loves and hates.)

1. Some of the things that God loves:

    a. Love, joy, peace, patience, kindness, goodness, faithfulness, gentleness, self control   —Galatians 5:22-23

    b. Faith   —Hebrews 11:6; Romans 4:19-22

    c. Heavenly-mindedness   —Colossians 3:1-3

    d. Care for the poor, widows and orphans   —Micah 6:8; James 1:27

    e. Cheerful giving   —2 Corinthians 9:7

    f. Worship   —John 4:24

    g. Humility and servanthood   —Philippians 2:1-8

    h. Forgiveness   —Ephesians 4:32

    i. Wisdom   —Proverbs 1–9

    j. Honor   —1 Timothy 5:17; 6:1

    k. Whatever is true, honorable, right, pure, lovely   —Philippians 4:8

The Rewards of Holiness

Lesson Six Notes

    l. Righteousness —Psalm 45:6-7

   m. Grace and peace —2 Timothy 2:1; 2 Peter 1:2

    n. Incense of prayer —Revelation 5:8

    o. Unity —Psalm 133

    p. Honesty and integrity —1 Peter 2:12

2. Some of the things that God hates:

    a. Pride, haughtiness, lies, hands that shed innocent blood, hearts that devise wicked plans, feet that run rapidly to evil, false witnesses who utter lies, one who spreads strife —Proverbs 6:16-19

    b. Immorality, impurity, sensuality, idolatry, sorcery, enmities, strife, jealousy, outbursts of anger, disputes, dissensions, factions, envying, drunkenness, carousing —Galatians 5:17-21

    c. Worldly-mindedness —Jude 18-19; 1 John 2:15-17

    d. Fornication, idolatry, adulterers, homosexuality, perversion, stealing, covetousness, reviling, swindling —1 Corinthians 6:9-10

    e. Hardness of heart, impurity, greed —Ephesians 4:18-19

    f. Religious spirit —Matthew 23

    g. Unbelief and disobedience —Hebrews 3-4

    h. Unforgiveness —Matthew 18:21-35

    i. Corrupt communication —Ephesians 4:29

    j. Coarse jesting and uncleanness —Ephesians 5:4

    k. Self righteousness —Romans 4; Galatians 3

3. As you draw close to God each day ask Him to:

    a. Reveal His heart to you concerning what He likes and why.

Lesson Six Notes

      b. Reveal His heart to you concerning what He doesn't like and why.

      c. Show you the things that you have done that He likes and why.

      d. Show you the things that you have done that He doesn't like and why.

4. What is your response?

D. Some of the Rewards of Holiness

1. Anointed with the oil of joy   —Psalm 45:6-7

2. Ascend unto the hill of the Lord   —Psalm 24:3-6

3. See the Lord   —Hebrews 12:14; Isaiah 35:2-8

4. Everlasting life   —Romans 6:22

5. Shining face   —Exodus 34:29-35; Matthew 17:1-2

6. Appearance of glory   —Isaiah 60:1-3

7. Established hearts in God   —1 Thessalonians 3:13

8. Experience Kingdom power   —Acts 1:8; Isaiah 35:2-10

9. Know the beauty of holiness   —1 Chronicles 16:29 (NKJV); Psalm 29:2 (NKJV)

10. Sent one   —Isaiah 6:1-9

11. The temple will fill with glory   —2 Chronicles 5

12. Victory and success   —Joshua 1:1-11; Deuteronomy 28:1-13

13. See wonders   —Joshua 3:5

14. Chosen to bring forth special purposes (i.e., Zacharius and Elizabeth)   —Luke 1:5-13

15. Prepares us as the bride   —Revelation 19:6-8

16. Prepares us to enjoy heavenly glory —Revelation 21:9-27

17. Blessed with heavenly blessing to the "utmost bound of the everlasting hills." —Genesis 49:22-26

E. A Prayer of Dedication

Father, I thank You that You have called me by name to know, to love and to serve You. This is a wonderful and very awesome invitation. With all my heart, I dedicate my spirit, soul and body to You, Holy Father, and I invite You to perform Your sanctifying work in my life.

I draw close into relationship and fellowship with You in the Holy Spirit. Teach me to love what You love and hate what You hate. Help me to experience a rich and glorious relationship with You. Grant unto me a spirit of wisdom and of revelation in the knowledge of Christ, His holiness, His love, and His wisdom that I might be filled with all the fullness of Your heavenly glory. Thank You, Father. Accept my life as a sacrifice that will bring forth a sweet aroma of Your presence in every place. In Jesus' name I dedicate myself unto Your holiness. AMEN.

Lesson Six Notes

LESSON SEVEN

DAILY DISCIPLINES FOR EXPERIENCING HEAVENLY GLORY

Our experience in the glory is led by the Holy Spirit and is born out of relationship with Him. Daily spiritual discipline is advantageous in that it helps us to position ourselves before Him and to focus our attention on His goodness towards us. The Bible teaches us to be disciplined and to bring our flesh under submission to the Spirit. Discipline fortifies our will and develops our character, but it does not produce the glory. Experience in the glory is never earned, it is simply a gift granted by His grace and goodness and received by faith. We can always anticipate the manifestation of the goodness of the Lord when we posture ourselves to receive.

"Then Moses said, 'I pray You, show me Your glory!' And He said, 'I Myself will make all My goodness pass before you, and will proclaim the name of the Lord before you.'"   —Exodus 33:18-19

The following are principles and preparations for worship, surrender and for experiencing the Father's heavenly glory. Make these principles personal through confession, meditation and response:

Lesson Seven Notes

1. I acknowledge that I have been born again. It is my spirit that is born again. In my spirit I have the very nature of Christ. I am in Christ in my spirit. I am one with Him for all eternity. This new birth is a gift. It cannot be earned but it is received by faith – it is the gift of eternal life – the life of Christ. As I acknowledge my born-again nature, I confess all that is true. I have the nature of Christ, I am forgiven, I am holy, I am full of wisdom and righteousness and power. I meditate on and confess all that I am and all that I have in my born-again spirit. This is the true *me*. My spirit man is to rule over my soul and over my body. It is not to be subdued, but it is to arise and shine and lead my soul and body. I bless my spirit man and set it apart to fulfill my Lord's purposes today.

2. I choose to lay down the rule of my soul life. I call my flesh, my carnal nature, crucified. I submit my soul to the rule of Christ within my born-again spirit man. I confess that my soul delights in submitting to the rule of Christ. My soul will not make its own decisions nor follow its own inclinations, but rather my soul nature submits to the life of Christ in my inner man.

3. I receive forgiveness for any area of my life that has transgressed the will and nature of God. My soul and body receive cleansing through the forgiving blood of Jesus. All my sins are forgiven. They have been removed as far as the east is from the west. Sin does not have dominion over my spirit, soul or body. I do not serve sin. I serve my God and all that He represents.

4. I consecrate my body, soul (including my mind, will, emotions, imagination, and affection), and spirit to the purposes of God. My entire being submits to the glory of God. I declare that my physical body is a container that reflects heavenly glory. The glory of the Lord shall appear upon me and nations and kings will be drawn to His salvation as a result. My entire being is fully influenced by the glory and presence of God.

Daily Disciplines for Experiencing Heavenly Glory

5. Like Moses, I enter the "tent of meeting" by faith. I choose to completely focus on the Lord and allow all the agenda and the busyness of the day to be laid down. I choose with expectancy to meet with the Lord.

6. I acknowledge my love and reverence for the Holy Spirit. He is my guide, my teacher, my helper, and my comforter. He leads me into truth and prepares me as a bride. He attaches Himself to me as an attendant who brings me to my final destination. He leads me daily into worship of Jesus and into experience of heavenly glory. I daily pray in tongues to build myself up in my spirit man. This fortifies me and enables me to be sensitive to the presence of the Lord and His Kingdom. As I pray in tongues I declare the mysteries of the Kingdom of God and proclaim His mighty deeds.

7. I make my soul drink daily of heavenly glory. I drink of the truth and allow my soul (mind, will, emotions, imagination, and affection) to receive of all that is in the deep well of my spirit. Through confession of who I am in Christ and what I have been given in the Kingdom, I wash my soul and see it renewed through the Word of God. This releases my soul to acknowledge heavenly glory. Daily, I confess the Word of God and allow my soul to drink of truth.

8. I study the Word daily and seek to know God in deeper ways. My soul loves His Word. It is a lamp unto my feet and a light unto my path. I do not stumble when I obey His Word. If I abide in Him and His Word abides in me then I will be fruitful and experience answers to prayer.

9. I worship Jesus in spirit and in truth. I acknowledge His worth and His value. I proclaim the glorious truth regarding my God and knit my heart together with Him in intimate love. The highest and holiest respect of my life belongs to Him and to none other. I behold His beauty and glory and exalt Him to the highest place in my life.

10. I engage in devotional and intercessory prayer while in His presence. I share my heart with the Lord and make my needs

Lesson Seven Notes

Lesson Seven Notes

known to Him. I also pray for the needs of others as the Holy Spirit directs, and I believe for the advancement of His Kingdom in the earth.

11. I wait on Him. I rest. I listen. I watch. What will He speak to me? What will He show me? He will reveal His heavenly glory to me. He will reveal His heart. I believe that He is speaking to me, meeting with me regardless of what I feel or experience in the natural. I believe by faith and receive by faith what He has promised me. I wait in expectancy for Him to bring fresh revelation and insight. I savor His presence and delight in what He shows me. I record in my journal the treasures that He reveals and I meditate on these things throughout the day.

12. I respond. I do the things that my Father shows me. Jesus said, "The Son can do nothing of Himself, unless it is something He sees the Father doing; for whatever the Father does, these things the Son also does in like manner."   —John 5:19
I, like my Savior, do the things that I see my Father doing. I obey His leading and commit myself to walking throughout my day in heavenly glory.

LESSON EIGHT

SPIRITUAL MAPPING: MAPPING THE THRONE ZONE

SPIRITUAL MAPPING – A DEFINITION

The term "spiritual mapping" was coined and became popular terminology in the body of Christ in the 1980s. It was a term mainly used to describe the study of geographical regions in areas of historical, political, and religious events in order to help determine "entry points" for demonic strongholds in those regions. It also embraces the study of godly heritage in order to aid in the discernment of the redemptive gifts in a region. Once an area was mapped out through in-depth research and study in museums, archives, newspapers, historical transcripts, etc., then intercession strategies were brought into place in order to bring cleansing and forgiveness to the land and its peoples. This process potentially produced faith and motivation in Christians to believe for the Holy Spirit to bring an outpouring of revival and harvest in their region.

While ministering in the United States in 2001, Jill Austin challenged me regarding this issue of spiritual mapping. Although she recognized its validity in the area of successful intercession and spiritual warfare, she questioned, "But how many have taken the time to map out heaven?" That question convicted me, so I began to pursue an in-depth

Lesson Eight Notes

study and meditation of the most accurate and only valid resource on the subject: the Scriptures themselves.

Through my studies I became convinced that our Father wants us to know what heaven looks like, what activities go on there, and who lives (or "hangs out") in His heavenly glory and presence. He not only wants us to know these things but He gives invitation to experience this heavenly glory, too. The Scriptures are the perfect and flawless account of such mapping. Explore heaven through study and experience ... and enjoy!

A. Introduction

1. The Scriptures tell us everything that we need to know about the heavenly realm. Use the Word of God to map out the "throne zone." There are over 750 references in the Bible concerning heaven, and over 200 of them refer to the place of God's abode in the highest heaven.

2. Our spirit man (born-again nature) is very acquainted with the "throne zone."

    "Which He brought about in Christ, when He raised Him from the dead and seated Him at His right hand in the heavenly places, far above all rule and authority and power and dominion, and every name that is named, not only in this age but also in the one to come ... and raised us up with Him, and seated us with Him in the heavenly places in Christ Jesus."
    —Ephesians 1:20-21; 2:6

3. Our souls and bodies are to be influenced and brought under the rule of our spirit man.

4. Our souls (mind, will, emotions, imaginations) are able to experience the influence of the truth and the Kingdom realm.

5. Sanctified will, mind, emotions, imagination, affections, and consecrated physical bodies can prepare and aid one to receive experiences of truth and the heavenly realm. (Note: the Holy

Spirit leads and directs us, but we prepare ourselves to receive of Him.)

6. Faith is the "connector" between truth and experience.

7. The Holy Spirit is our teacher and guide into all truth and experience.

B. A Spiritual Exercise – Biblical Visions of the Throne Room

"Bodily exercise is all right, but spiritual exercise is much more important and is a tonic for all you do. So exercise yourself spiritually and practice being a better Christian, because that will help you not only now in this life, but in the next life too."
—1 Timothy 4:8 LB

"But solid food is for the mature, who because of practice have their senses trained to discern good and evil."   —Hebrews 5:14

"Now set your sights on the rich treasures and joys of heaven.... Let heaven fill your thoughts."   —Colossians 3:1-2 LB

The Bible is full of information regarding heaven and the throne room. The following portions of Scripture will be significant in your study and discovery of what the heavenly realm is like:

Exodus 24:9-11; Isaiah 6:1-8; Ezekiel 1; Daniel 7:9-10; Revelation 1:10-16; 4–5; 19:1-16; 20:11-12; 21-22:7

Preparation

The following is an overview of principles that will help prepare your heart in holiness and readiness to engage in spiritual mapping. Consecration, examination of the Scriptures, and openness to experience are all involved in mapping the throne zone.

1. Prepare your heart by worshipping the Lord.

Lesson Eight Notes

2. Invite the Holy Spirit to convict you of unconfessed sin. —Psalm 24:3-4

3. Confess, repent and receive forgiveness for sin. —1 John 1:9

4. Commit your spirit, soul and body to the direction of the Holy Spirit.

5. Invite the Holy Spirit to reveal truth to you concerning the throne room and heavenly glory.

6. Read the Scriptures (try one portion at a time).

7. Meditate on the Scriptures

8. Submit your soul (thoughts, emotions, and imagination) to the vision portrayed in the Scripture, and ask the Holy Spirit to grant wisdom and revelation to your heart.

9. Believe in the reality of the vision that is found in the Word as you read it in Scripture. In other words, what you are reading is not a fantasy or someone's own thoughts about heaven, but is truth from God.

10. Receive by faith the experience of "seeing" and "hearing" the visions of the throne room that are found in the Word of God. Invite the Holy Spirit to bring to your imagination, your thoughts, and your emotions the experience of that which is true according to Scripture. Be open also to other portions of Scripture that the Holy Spirit might quicken you to study. Journal the insights and revelations that you believe you have received. Confirm those insights and/or revelations with the Scriptures.

11. Soak in the beauty of the vision you have seen in the Scripture and any experience that the Holy Spirit has granted you. Thank Him for leading you into such glorious truth.

12. Glorify Jesus and honor your Heavenly Father who has shown you such kindness. Worship with increased passion and focus.

Lesson Eight Notes

Mapping the Throne Room – A Practical Study and Exercise

Study, Meditate, Pray, and Journal

C. The Open Door —Revelation 4:1

1. The Door
   a. Into heaven
   b. Into end-time revelation
2. An invitation is given
   a. To John
   b. To Moses and the 70 (corporate)
   c. To us?
   d. RSVP

D. Behold, a Throne —Revelation 4:2

1. "In the Spirit"
   a. Holy Spirit directed experience (praying in tongues can build up the spirit man)
2. God's sovereign dominion and authority
   a. Set in heaven

E. One Who Sat On the Throne —Revelation 4:2

1. Revelation of the Father   —Revelation 4
2. Revelation of the Son   —Revelation 5
3. The Ultimate Ruler of the universe is revealed.

Lesson Eight Notes

  a. He was like jasper and sardius in appearance.
 —Revelation 4:3

  b. Clothed in light   —Psalm 104:2; 1 Timothy 6:16

  c. Amber color with fire from the loins up and fire from the loins down   —Ezekiel 1:27

4. Appearance of the throne

  a. Ablaze with fire; wheels of fire; river of fire proceeding from it   —Daniel 7:9-10

  b. Jasper, sardius   —Revelation 4:3

  c. Throne like sapphire stone   —Ezekiel 1:26

  d. Rainbow like emerald   —Revelation 4:3; Ezekiel 1:28

  e. Lightnings, thunderings and voices proceed from it
 —Revelation 4:5

  f. Sea of glass like crystal before the throne   —Revelation 4:6

F. BEINGS IN HEAVEN (NON-EXHAUSTIVE)

1. The twenty four elders   —Revelation 4:4

  a. Sitting on thrones

  b. Crowns of gold

  c. Make decisions

2. The Seven Spirits of God   —Revelation 4:5

  a. The Holy Spirit

  b. Before the throne

  c. The Spirit of the Lord, Spirit of Wisdom, Spirit of Understanding; Spirit of Might; Spirit of Knowledge, Spirit of the Fear of the Lord   —Isaiah 11:2

3. The Living Creatures   —Revelation 4:6-9

    a. Creatures like: a lion, a calf, an eagle, and a man

    b. Six wings

    c. Eyes around and within

4. The Seraphim   —Isaiah 6

    a. Fiery ones

    b. Six wings

    c. Minister at the altar

5. The Cherubim   —Ezekiel 1

    a. Over the mercy seat   —Exodus 25:18-22

    b. Stewards of the glory   —Ezekiel 10:1-20; 11:22

    c. Jesus sits between the cherubim   —Psalm 99:1

6. Myriads of angels   —Revelation 5:11

7. The great cloud of witnesses   —Hebrews 12:1

8. Horses, chariots   —Revelation 19:11,14; Psalm 68:17

G. Activities in Heaven (non-exhaustive)

1. Worship   —Revelation 4–5

2. Harps   —Revelation 5:8

3. Incense (prayers of the saints)   —Revelation 5:8

4. Purging iniquity   —Isaiah 6

5. Eating and drinking   —Exodus 24:11

6. Joy and laughter   — Psalm 2:4; Luke 15:10

7. Blow trumpets   —Revelation 4

8. Banquet   —Revelation 19:7-9

9. Open seals and release judgments   —Revelation 5-20

Lesson Eight Notes

H. Throne Room Perspective

1. Vital perspective for the last days (book of Revelation)

    a. Keep faith and focus.

    b. Do not grow weary in well doing.

   Seek those things above where Christ is seated.   —Colossians 3:1-2

    c. Holiness

    d. Spiritual blessings

    e. Eternal perspective

LESSON NINE

HEARING THE VOICE OF GOD

A. Does God Speak to His People?

1. My sheep hear My voice   —John 10:27

2. Hear what the Spirit says to the church   —Revelation 2–3

B. What Are Some of the Ways That God Speaks to His People?

1. Still small voice (words or thoughts)

2. Through the eyes of our heart with "thought pictures"

3. Through the Scriptures

4. Through creation

5. Through other believers

6. Through trials and testings

7. Audible voice

8. Inner audible voice

Lesson Nine Notes

9. Dreams
10. Day dreams
11. Open eye vision
12. Closed eye vision
13. Open eye "spiritual" vision
14. Colors
15. Symbols (i.e., animals, flowers, foods, objects)
16. Through prophecy
17. Through words of knowledge
18. Through angelic visitation
19. Through feelings

Lesson Ten

Experiencing the Third Heaven

Part One

"After these things I looked, and behold, a door standing open in heaven, and the first voice which I had heard, like the sound of a trumpet speaking with me, said, 'Come up here, and I will show you what must take place after these things.'"
—Revelation 4:1-2

A. What Is the Spiritual Realm?

The "unseen," eternal realm.

"While we look not at the things which are seen, but at the things which are not seen; for the things which are seen are temporal, but the things which are not seen are eternal."   —2 Corinthians 4:18

A scriptural example of "seeing" into the spiritual realm.

> So he said, "Go and see where he is, that I may send and take him." And it was told him, saying, "Behold, he is in Dothan."

Lesson Ten Notes

> He sent horses and chariots and a great army there, and they came by night and surrounded the city. Now when the attendant of the man of God had risen early and gone out, behold, an army with horses and chariots was circling the city. And his servant said to him, "Alas, my master! What shall we do?"
>
> So he answered, "Do not fear, for those who are with us are more than those who are with them."
>
> Then Elisha prayed, and said, "O Lord, I pray, open his eyes, that he may see. And the Lord opened the servant's eyes and he saw; and behold, the mountain was full of horses and chariots of fire all around Elisha. —2 Kings 6:13-17

Things that are seen were brought forth first through the Word of God which was spoken in the unseen or spiritual realm.

> By faith we understand that the worlds were prepared by the word of God, so that what is seen was not made out of things which are visible. —Hebrews 11:3

B. Two Kingdoms in the Spiritual Realm

> Then a demon-possessed man who was blind and mute was brought to Jesus, and He healed him, so that the mute man spoke and saw. All the crowds were amazed, and were saying, "This man cannot be the son of David, can he?"
>
> But when the Pharisees heard this, they said, "This man casts out demons only by Beelzebul the ruler of the demons." And knowing their thoughts Jesus said to them, "Any kingdom divided against itself is laid waste; and any city or house divided against itself will not stand. If Satan casts out Satan, he is divided against himself; how then will his kingdom stand? If I by Beelzebul cast out demons, by whom do your sons cast them out? For this reason they will be your judges. But if I cast out demons by the Spirit of God, then the kingdom of God has come upon you." —Matthew 12:22-28

Giving thanks to the Father, who has qualified us to share in the inheritance of the saints in Light. For He rescued us from the domain of darkness, and transferred us to the kingdom of His beloved Son. —Colossians 1:12-13

Therefore, since we receive a kingdom which cannot be shaken, let us show gratitude, by which we may offer to God an acceptable service with reverence and awe.
—Hebrews 12:28

Kingdom of God

1. Jesus has rule   —Matthew 28:18; Philippians 2:9-11
2. Angels   —Hebrews 1:13-14
3. Redeemed   —Colossians 1:12-13
4. Law of the spirit of life   —Romans 8:2

Kingdom of Satan

1. satan has rule   —2 Corinthians 4:4; 1 John 5:19
2. demons   —Matthew 12:22-28
3. unredeemed   —Ephesians 2:1-3
4. law of sin and death   —Romans 8:2

No Time – No Distance in the Spirit Realm

Examples: the visions of Ezekiel, the transport of Phillip, the experiences in the glory realm by John in the book of Revelations; Paul's experiences in the third heaven.

Lesson Ten Notes

C. What Is Heaven?

The subject of heaven is a significant topic in the Scriptures with more than 750 references found in the Bible. Over 250 of these references relate to the "abode of God."

From Strong's Concordance – Hebrew

08064 ~ymf shamayim shaw-mah'-yim dual of an unused singular hmf shameh shaw-meh'

1. heaven, heavens, sky

    1a. visible heavens, sky

        1a1. as abode of the stars

        1a2. as the visible universe, the sky, atmosphere, etc.

    1b. heaven (as the abode of God)

From Strong's Concordance – Greek

3772 ouranoj ouranos oo-ran-os'

1. the vaulted expanse of the sky with all things visible in it

    1a. the universe, the world

    1b. the aerial heavens or sky, the region where the clouds and the tempests gather, and where thunder and lightning are produced

    1c. the sidereal or starry heavens

2. the region above the sidereal heavens, the seat of order of things eternal and consummately perfect where God dwells and other heavenly beings

D. What Is the Third Heaven?

The third heaven is a scriptural term found once in Scripture. It is used to describe the abode of God. The throne room is in this realm.

I know a man in Christ who fourteen years ago – whether in the body I do not know, or out of the body I do not know, God knows – such a man was caught up to the third heaven. —2 Corinthians 12:2

Thus the heavens and the earth were completed, and all their hosts. —Genesis 2:1

Behold, to the Lord your God belong heaven and the highest heavens, the earth and all that is in it. —Deuteronomy 10:14

First and Second Heaven?

a. First – earth's atmosphere – stars, moon, sun —Psalm 8:3

b. Second – realm of the angelic and demonic —Daniel 10; fallen angels realm —Ezekiel 8:3

Third Heaven?

a. Highest heaven?

b. Place of Christ's rule and authority?

c. Paul was taken there —2 Corinthians 12:2

d. Paul called it "Paradise" —2 Corinthians 12:4

Paradise: 3857 paradeisoj paradeisos par-ad'-i-sos (Strong's-Greek)

– the part of Hades

– the upper regions of the heavens

– heaven

<3857> And [Jesus] said to him, "Truly I say to you, today you shall be with Me in Paradise." —Luke 23:43

Lesson Ten Notes

<3857> And I know how such a man ... was caught up into Paradise and heard inexpressible words, which a man is not permitted to speak. —2 Corinthians 12:3-4

<3857> He who has an ear, let him hear what the Spirit says to the churches To him who overcomes, I will grant to eat of the tree of life which is in the Paradise of God. —Revelation 2:7

Is Paradise/Third Heaven, the Throne Room Level of Heaven?

Quite possibly.

Paul called "Paradise" the third heaven.

There are no other specific higher levels of heaven mentioned in the Scriptures.

Jesus is the "tree of life" which is in the midst of Paradise.

Jesus is seated at the right hand of the Father on His throne.

Is It Possible That Paradise (referred to by Paul as the third heaven) Is Only One Level of the Heavens and There Are Still Levels Beyond?

Scriptures do not give reference to this.

It is wise to use Bible terminology when describing spiritual experience and to confirm experiences in God with the validation of His Word. To use terminology of "higher heavens" (i.e., 7th heaven) would be extra-biblical.

E. Ascending and Descending Into the Heavens

1. Angels

   [Jacob] had a dream, and behold, a ladder was set on the earth with its top reaching to heaven; and behold, the angels of God were ascending and descending on it. —Genesis 28:12

> And He said to him, "Truly, truly, I say to you, you will see the heavens opened and the angels of God ascending and descending on the Son of Man."   —John 1:51

2. Paul   —2 Corinthians 12:2-4

3. John   —Revelation 4:1-2 (from a vision to the throne room)

4. Isaiah   —Isaiah 6

5. David   —Psalm 139:7-8

6. Moses   —Exodus 24:9-11

7. Jesus

> Therefore Jesus answered and was saying to them, "Truly, truly, I say to you, the Son can do nothing of Himself, unless it is something He sees the Father doing; for whatever the Father does, these things the Son also does in like manner. For the Father loves the Son, and shows Him all things that He Himself is doing; and the Father will show Him greater works than these, so that you will marvel.   —John 5:19-20

Jesus engaged in two types of ascending:

1. "Ascending in devotional prayer and worship."

2. Historical ascension of Christ.

F. What Is the Kingdom of Heaven?

A Kingdom is a place where a *King* has rule. The Kingdom of God is His domain of rule.

There are 32 New Testament references to the Kingdom of Heaven.

Matthew 3:2; 4:17

Lesson Ten Notes

Lesson Ten Notes

G. What Does It Mean to Be "A New Creation in Christ"?

> Therefore if anyone is in Christ, he is a new creature; the old things passed away; behold, new things have come.
> —2 Corinthians 5:17

> Now may the God of peace Himself sanctify you entirely; and may your spirit and soul and body be preserved complete, without blame at the coming of our Lord Jesus Christ.
> —1 Thessalonians 5:23

Body – relates to the physical

Soul – relates to the emotions, reasonings, will, relational realm

Spirit – relates to the spirit realm

> That which is born of the flesh is flesh; and that which is born of the Spirit is spirit.   —John 3:6

Our born-again spirits are sensitive to the Spirit of God, and they contain the nature of God and the life of Christ.

The Scripture says that we are "in Christ" if we are a believer:

> And raised us up with Him, and seated us with Him in the heavenly places in Christ Jesus.   —Ephesians 2:6

> For we are His workmanship, created in Christ Jesus for good works, which God prepared beforehand so that we would walk in them.   —Ephesians 2:10

> But now in Christ Jesus you who formerly were far off have been brought near by the blood of Christ.   —Ephesians 2:13

H. Are Believers Able to Experience the Spirit Realm?

Yes. Our spirits were created in us to make us sensitive to that realm. There are many examples throughout Scripture of God's people having spiritual experiences. Even though each individual will have different experiences, depending on the leading of the Holy Spirit, all believers are invited to enjoy the reality of the Lord and His Kingdom.

I. Are Believers Able to Access the Third Heaven Realm?

1. On the basis of being "in Christ" (If Christ is seated on the throne in the highest heaven, and if we are in Christ, then we also in our spirits would be able to access the throne room position by faith.)

    That the God of our Lord Jesus Christ, the Father of glory, may give to you a spirit of wisdom and of revelation in the knowledge of Him. I pray that the eyes of your heart may be enlightened, so that you will know what is the hope of His calling, what are the riches of the glory of His inheritance in the saints,

    And what is the surpassing greatness of His power toward us who believe. These are in accordance with the working of the strength of His might which He brought about in Christ, when He raised Him from the dead and seated Him at His right hand in the heavenly places, far above all rule and authority and power and dominion, and every name that is named, not only in this age but also in the one to come. And He put all things in subjection under His feet, and gave Him as head over all things to the church, which is His body, the fullness of Him who fills all in all.   —Ephesians 1:17-23

    Even when we were dead in our transgressions, made us alive together with Christ (by grace you have been saved), and raised us up with Him, and seated us with Him in the heavenly places in Christ Jesus.   —Ephesians 2:5-6

    According to the preceding Scripture, we are already positioned in the throne room (we believe that another term for the *throne room* is "third heaven"). It is simply a matter of becoming aware of this through the opening of our understanding by revelation of the Word.

Lesson Ten Notes

Lesson Ten Notes

> After these things I looked, and behold, a door standing open in heaven, and the first voice which I had heard, like the sound of a trumpet speaking with me, said, "Come up here, and I will show you what must take place after these things." Immediately I was in the Spirit; and behold, a throne was standing in heaven, and One sitting on the throne. —Revelation 4:1-2

2. We are citizens of heaven.

> But you have come to Mount Zion and to the city of the living God, the heavenly Jerusalem, and to myriads of angels, to the general assembly and church of the firstborn who are enrolled in heaven, and to God, the Judge of all, and to the spirits of the righteous made perfect, and to Jesus, the mediator of a new covenant, and to the sprinkled blood, which speaks better than the blood of Abel. —Hebrews 12:22-24

> So then you are no longer strangers and aliens, but you are fellow citizens with the saints, and are of God's household. —Ephesians 2:19

> But as it is, they desire a better country, that is, a heavenly one. Therefore God is not ashamed to be called their God; for He has prepared a city for them. —Hebrews 11:16

> "In My Father's house are many dwelling places; if it were not so, I would have told you; for I go to prepare a place for you. If I go and prepare a place for you, I will come again and receive you to Myself, that where I am, there you may be also. And you know the way where I am going." —John 14:2-4

J. Are Believers Allowed to Or Encouraged to Access the Third Heaven?

Access (Websters Dictionary):

1. the act of coming toward or near to; approach

2. a way or means of approaching, getting, using, etc.

3. the right to enter, approach, or use, admittance

4. increase or growth

Therefore if you have been raised up with Christ, keep seeking the things above, where Christ is, seated at the right hand of God. Set your mind on the things above, not on the things that are on earth. For you have died and your life is hidden with Christ in God.   —Colossians 3:1-3

After these things I looked, and behold, a door standing open in heaven, and the first voice which I had heard, like the sound of a trumpet speaking with me, said, "Come up here, and I will show you what must take place after these things." Immediately I was in the Spirit; and behold, a throne was standing in heaven, and One sitting on the throne.   —Revelation 4:1-2

Therefore let us draw near with confidence to the throne of grace, so that we may receive mercy and find grace to help in time of need.   —Hebrews 4:16

For Christ did not enter a holy place made with hands, a mere copy of the true one, but into heaven itself, now to appear in the presence of God for us.   —Hebrews 9:24

Therefore, brethren, since we have confidence to enter the holy place by the blood of Jesus, by a new and living way which He inaugurated for us through the veil, that is, His flesh, and since we have a great priest over the house of God, let us draw near with a sincere heart in full assurance of faith.
—Hebrews 10:19-22

K. What Is the Difference Between a Sovereign Act of God and a Faith Act of a Believer?

1. Sovereign Acts: God initiates.

    Why? Usually as a forerunner or as a sign and wonder to encourage believers to walk in faith.

Lesson Ten Notes

Lesson Ten Notes

2. Faith Acts: The believer accesses the promises of covenant by their faith.

"The righteous man shall live by faith."   —Romans 1:17

All the supernatural gifts and abilities of the Holy Spirit and the Kingdom are operated by faith. There are times while operating in the prophetic that the "word of the Lord" will come to an individual. This is a sovereign act initiated by God. The individual wasn't looking for it or seeking after it.

There are other times that an individual will step out in faith to receive a prophetic word. This is a faith act, and this step of faith can secure the opening of our understanding to biblical truth concerning the Kingdom realm and third heaven.

This does not mean that man's will determines or maneuvers an experience. True faith comes as a result of submission to the leading of the Holy Spirit. Therefore, man can "will" to submit to the Holy Spirit and the Word of God. He can "will" to "seek those things which are above, where Christ is, sitting at the right hand of God" (Colossians 3:1), but must allow the Holy Spirit's leading through the experience.

It is equally important to note that a believer cannot "legally" access another person's spiritual experience by faith (not even the experience of a Bible character) unless the Holy Spirit specifically reveals this. Believers can, however, access the realities and the promises of the Kingdom and heavenly realm as they are led by the Spirit of God.

For example, we know that we as believer's can have a worship or prayer experience in the throne room. The Scripture says that we are seated there with Christ and that we can boldly come before the throne of grace. The Scripture does not say that we will have the exact same experience as Paul or John.

It is also important to note that a sovereignly initiated act does not necessarily carry more weight in Kingdom experience than an act that is accessed by the faith of a believer. Let me give you an example. I have had a number of sovereignly initiated visions and spiritual encounters. Two specific experiences were extremely vivid and granted me revelation of God's glorious heaven. They impacted my life and they have also impacted many other lives as I shared the experiences and what I learned from them.

These experiences, however, do not carry necessarily more Kingdom or personal impact than the numerous experiences I have accessed by faith. Let me give you a biblical example: The woman with the issue of blood was determined in her own heart to be healed. She pressed in through the crowd and grabbed hold of Jesus' garment. She drew virtue from Him and was healed. Jesus commended her for her faith. He did not initiate her healing. She received by faith. Now, that particular faith act of the woman carries much more influence and effect for the advancement of the Kingdom than my two sovereignly initiated third heaven experiences. Why? Because God chose to set her faith experience in Scripture and use it to encourage those who would read the account all through church history.

Hebrews 11 lists many heroes of the faith. From what we read in the Scriptures, some individuals listed there did not have any sovereignly initiated spiritual experiences. But they did experience the Lord by faith and continue to have influence to this day.

Experiences with God that are either sovereignly initiated or accessed by faith are both valid. But they are received differently. We often put less value on something that has been accessed by faith, but this should not be the case. The sphere of influence and the weight of the experience will often depend on the Lord's placement of it within the realm of time.

Lesson Ten Notes

Lesson Eleven

Experiencing the Third Heaven

Part Two: Activation

A. How Do We Experience the Spiritual Realm?

1. All experience in the Kingdom must be based on the authority of God's Word and His covenant promises (note: not on the basis of another's experience – not even a bible character's experience).

   The Father loves the Son and has given all things into His hand.   —John 3:35

   We are joint heirs with Christ, therefore all things have been given unto us.

2. Believers are "in Christ" and are given:

   a. Every spiritual blessing in the heavenly places.
   —Ephesians 1:3

   b. Everything needed to live a godly and fulfilling life.
   —2 Peter 1:2-4

Lesson Eleven Notes

3. Believers experience the spiritual realm by faith.

    All things in the Kingdom are able to be brought into our experience through faith in the Word and promises of God (i.e., salvation, healing, freedom) as the Spirit leads. —Hebrews 11:6; Mark 11:24

    So the other disciples were saying to him, "We have seen the Lord!" But he said to them, "Unless I see in His hands the imprint of the nails, and put my finger into the place of the nails, and put my hand into His side, I will not believe."

    After eight days His disciples were again inside, and Thomas with them. Jesus came, the doors having been shut, and stood in their midst and said, "Peace be with you."

    Then He said to Thomas, "Reach here with your finger, and see My hands; and reach here your hand and put it into My side; and do not be unbelieving, but believing."

    Thomas answered and said to Him, "My Lord and my God!" Jesus said to him, "Because you have seen Me, have you believed? Blessed are they who did not see, and yet believed." —John 20:25-29

4. Our spirits were created to help us relate to the Kingdom realm.

    Our spirits need to be exercised. In our western culture we are often diligent at strengthening our physical bodies through weightlifting, exercise, health food products, and vitamins. Our intellect is exercised through an emphasis on education. Our emotions receive a great deal of focus through self-help programs and inner healing. But there is little promotion of exercise that would develop healthy and sensitive spirits. Much of the western church is afraid of spiritual life and experience. We tend to lean on logic; we experience very little in the area of spiritual life on a general corporate level within the church.

    There are many teachers in the body of Christ who activate the prophetic gifts, song writing, intercession, poetic, art, and dance expressions, and worship experience, by "consecrating" and "activating" the mind and the "eyes of the heart" (imagination). This act of separation unto the Lord brings these organs of the soul into submission to the Holy Spirit and enhances spiritual sensitivity. This is done through a variety of activation exercises and, as a result, participating believers are becoming more Kingdom-sensitive, able to release increased God-inspired creativity. This type of consecration and activation can also be applied in accessing the Bible truths concerning other promises in the Kingdom realm (see more under #6 Sanctified Imagination. Also review Lesson Nine on *Hearing the Voice of God*).

The born again spirit man is already very acquainted with the Kingdom realm. The spirit man is completely united with the Lord, His covenant promises, and His purposes. It is important then that we learn to follow the leading of our born-again spiritual nature and allow our souls and bodies to become sensitive to all that is within us of the Christ-life.

5. Under the complete control of the Holy Spirit (invite His leading – submit to Him and to truth)

   Read John 14. The Holy Spirit is our Helper, our "paracletos," and comes alongside to lead and guide us into all truth.

   When we engage in Kingdom life and experience, we must be in complete submission to the Holy Spirit, allowing Him to lead, teach, and convict us. In no way are we to pave our own way into the heavenlies. Jesus is the Way and the Holy Spirit is our guide. Our own soulish tendencies to rule in Kingdom experiences must be laid down.

6. Sanctified Imagination – the eyes of our heart (understanding).

   That the God of our Lord Jesus Christ, the Father of glory, may give to you a spirit of wisdom and of revelation in the knowledge of Him.

   I pray that the eyes of your heart may be enlightened, so that you will know what is the hope of His calling, what are the

Lesson Eleven Notes

riches of the glory of His inheritance in the saints, and what is the surpassing greatness of His power toward us who believe. These are in accordance with the working of the strength of His might which He brought about in Christ, when He raised Him from the dead and seated Him at His right hand in the heavenly places.   —Ephesians 1:17-20

From Strong's:

Understanding

1271 dianoia dianoia dee-an'-oy-ah

AV – mind, understanding, imagination

1. the mind as a faculty of understanding, feeling, desiring
2. understanding
3. mind, i.e., spirit, way of thinking and feeling
4. thoughts, either good or bad

Much of our spiritual revelation is fed into our imagination or mind. We are oftentimes afraid of using our mind or imagination to receive revelation from the Lord. Imagination (the eyes of our heart) is, however, frequently used by the Lord to enable believers to envision Kingdom truth.

The activation of the sanctified imagination during times of worship, Bible reading and prayer is very common historically in the biblical meditation and contemplation practices of western Christianity.

7. By reason of practice

But solid food is for the mature, who because of practice have their senses trained to discern good and evil.   —Hebrews 5:14

Even so faith, if it has no works, is dead, being by itself. But someone may well say, "You have faith and I have works; show me your faith without the works, and I will show you my faith by my works."   —James 2:17-18

EXPERIENCING THE THIRD HEAVEN PART TWO

Lesson Eleven Notes

Activation is valid.

Worship. Worship is a wonderful place to activate faith. Begin to exalt the Lord and invite the Lord to reveal aspects of His beauty, glory and awesomeness. Reach out to receive revelation of His magnificence and then respond by worshipping Him with greater abandonment.

Prayer. Prayer time is also a good time to activate. "Come boldly to the throne of grace" (Hebrews 4:16 NKJV). By faith, stand in boldness before the throne of grace and petition the Lord.

Bible Reading: Meditate on the promises of God and seek the Scriptures to see the reality of the Kingdom of God. Invite the Lord to give you revelation of His glory and Kingdom splendor. Allow your mind, imagination, and attention to focus on "things above, where Christ is, seated at the right hand of God" (Colossians 3:1).

The benefits of journaling: You will find that as you journal what you see, hear, and experience in the Lord that it seals, so to speak, what you are encountering. Many times in Scripture the prophets were told to write what they saw or experienced. Meditate on the things that the Lord gives you throughout the day.

B. ARE THERE EXAMPLES OF GOD ENCOURAGING PEOPLE INTO THE GLORY/HEAVENLY REALM?

1. Moses – on Mount Sinai   —Exodus 24

2. Jesus – invited three disciples up to the mountain where He was transfigured. Peter, James and John experienced the spiritual/glory realm and heard the audible voice of God from heaven. This was Jesus' invitation – He "took them" into the experience (en masse – all of them)

Lesson Eleven Notes

C. Are There Possible Dangers of Seeking Kingdom Experiences? Yes!! Beware!

1. Witchcraft and Occultism

   Any manipulation or activity operated in the spirit realm that is not under the rule of Christ is witchcraft ...which is a work of the flesh (under the influence of man's fallen nature) and is a forbidden practice in Scripture.

   Be careful regarding "guided imagery." This is where someone else tells you what to see. This can be manipulation. Stay in complete submission to the Holy Spirit. —Deuteronomy 18:10-14; Galatians 5:17-25

2. Idolatry and Fascination

   "And beware not to lift up your eyes to heaven and see the sun and the moon and the stars, all the host of heaven, and be drawn away and worship them and serve them, those which the Lord your God has allotted to all the peoples under the whole heaven." —Deuteronomy 4:19

   Then I fell at his feet to worship him. But he said to me, "Do not do that; I am a fellow servant of yours and your brethren who hold the testimony of Jesus; worship God. For the testimony of Jesus is the spirit of prophecy." —Revelation 19:10

3. Experience orientation which causes imbalance.

   When a believer begins to get too focused on spiritual experiences, he/she can begin to believe that the experiences are what produces spiritual maturity, rather than pure devotion, faith and obedience to the Word of God. Our experience is simply a dimension of our wholehearted relationship with the Lord. Experience flows out of our worship, sole devotion to the Lord, and our radical commitment to Kingdom life. If we worship experience itself rather than the One whom we long to share experience with, then we fall into idolatry, and the way we relate to life and to others becomes imbalanced. (See the Appendix, "Nuts, Flakes, and Weirdos")

4. Pride and self exaltation

   Paul —2 Corinthians 12:1-7

   Peter —Matthew 17:1-8

   Lucifer —Isaiah 14:12-14

5. Touched but not changed

   Example: Israel —Luke 19:41-44

6. Error and deception

   Entering into experience without a proper and complete foundation in the Word of God can sometimes open the door to error and deception. Good solid Bible teaching should accompany spiritual experiences.

D. Concluding Questions Unto Evaluation

1. Is it scriptural that believers/characters recorded in the Bible have had experience in the spiritual/kingdom realm?

2. Is it scriptural that believers/characters recorded in the Bible have had experiences in the third heaven?

3. Is it scriptural that all New Testament born-again believers today are "in Christ"?

4. Is it scriptural that Christ is seated in the highest heaven above all other authority and dominions?

5. Is it true according to Scripture that if believers are in Christ, they also are seated with Him/in Him in the heavenly places?

6. Is it true that the righteous one lives by his faith in the promises of God and must access the life of Christ by faith?

7. Is it true that all the spiritual blessings in heavenly places have already been given to believers through the work of the cross?

Lesson Eleven Notes

8. Is it true that believers through faith may access all the spiritual blessings promised to us in the new covenant?

9. Is it possible according to Scripture to have the eyes of our understanding (imagination/spirit/mind) opened to see into the Kingdom realm?

10. Is it possible according to Scripture for believers to grow in spiritual sensitivity and discernment by reason of practice?

11. Do you believe that there is no distance or time in the spirit realm?

12. Should all Kingdom experience be based on, and founded on, scriptural truth?

13. Should good instruction on new creation realities/the gifts/spiritual experiences, etc., be well taught within the church as part of the equipping process?

14. Should spiritual experiences be well pastored?

15. Is it wise to invalidate what we don't understand if it is backed up by Scripture?

16. Do we see invitations in the Scripture to enter into Kingdom experience?

17. Where do we go from here?

E. Getting Prepared for Activation

Questions:

1. Are you born-again?

2. Are you willing to give yourself completely to the Lord in spirit, soul and body?

3. Have you repented of all known sin and received forgiveness?

4. Have you renounced any previous alliances or experiences in the occult, new age or false religious groups or practices?

5. Are you willing to believe the truth of God's Word even more than any experience that you might or might not encounter in your mind, emotions, or physical body?

6. Do you believe that the Lord desires to give you experience in His Kingdom and throne room (heavenly places/third heaven)?

7. Are you willing to completely yield to the Holy Spirit and His leading?

8. Are you willing to increase and grow in your worship, devotion, and service of Jesus?

Spiritual Exercises to build up your spirit man.

Note: These exercises are not necessarily an experience in the realities of the Kingdom, but they will prepare your being to be sensitive to the leading of the Holy Spirit.

1. Sanctify your entire being and especially your thoughts, emotions, physical body and imagination (eyes of your heart). Ask forgiveness for any vain or unclean thoughts, feelings or imaginations that you've allowed in your life.

2. Take a portion of Scripture, such as Revelation 4–5, and begin to submit your mind and imagination to the appearance of the throne room.

3. Pray in tongues – this builds up your spiritual sensitivity.

4. Worship Jesus – focus on Jesus as you worship.

5. Confess the Word of God daily. This strengthens your spirit and renews your mind according to covenant promises.

6. Choose to believe that you already are living in the heavenly realm with Christ in your spirit.

Activation.

1. Focus on Jesus and His heavenly glory. Worship Him, adore Him.

Lesson Eleven Notes

2. Believe that your spirit is one with Him and that you are with Him in the throne room, seated with Him. This is based on the truth of the Word of God.

3. Invite the Holy Spirit to lead you into experience in heavenly glory.

4. Operate in rest and in faith. Allow your imagination, your mind, your emotions and your body to submit to the Holy Spirit and to what He desires to reveal to you. There are a number of experiences that you might have. You might experience a faint picture in your mind or a brilliant open vision. You might have the still small voice of God impart a thought to your mind or you might hear an audible voice. Most of your encounters in the glory realm will be imparted to your mind and imagination. Meditate on what He is showing you and lean into His love and into anything that He is leading you into. Don't be afraid to ask Him questions while you are in the midst of experience – this is about relationship.

5. Take note of what He is showing you and try to remember it for later. Follow-up on Scripture studies to verify what you have experienced. Oftentimes you will see things in symbolic form such as colors, flowers, animals, numbers. Later, pray about what the Lord was trying to reveal to you through this.

6. If it seems that you are not receiving, remember that you actually are "in your spirit." Rest in that fact and rejoice in the wonderful truths concerning your new nature and your position in heaven. Walk by faith and not by sight. Your experience by faith is just as valid as one whose body and soul are experiencing glory.

7. Fellowship with the Holy Spirit following your experience. Dialogue with Him. Journal. Build a strong personal relationship with Him.

8. Glorify Jesus. Remember, that all experience in the King-

dom will lead you to adore the King. Worship and exalt Him with all your heart.

9. Remember that you are able to access the glory realm whenever you desire. Throughout the day, allow your thoughts to meditate on the beauty of Jesus and the glory of heaven.

10. Ask the Lord to show you what to deposit in the world around you (i.e., His love, mercy, truth). He might give you specific mandates. If so, obey Him and be blessed in His service. Remember – you are loved!

Lesson Eleven Notes

Lesson Twelve

Angelic Majesties

In God's Kingdom, He has created angelic beings who serve Him and His purposes. As covenant believers, these angelic majesties are sent to minister to us. Throughout the Bible, you will find a great deal of teaching about angels and the way they interface with man.

Prior to any significant Kingdom event, you will often find the increased appearance of angels. All believers have the ability to see angels through the eye of their spirit. We have been given the gift of the discerning of spirits so that we may discern the presence of angels and the presence of God, as well as discerning evil spirits from the kingdom of darkness. The gift of the discerning of spirits is within every believer – it is a gift of the Holy Spirit. If you have the Holy Spirit within you, you have His gifts.

Many believers might encounter visitations from angels in their lives, just like Abraham, Jacob, Isaiah, Ezekiel, Mary, Joseph, John and numerous others.

Definition of *angel* – messenger, representative, "dispatch as a deputy."

Read Hebrews 1.

Lesson Twelve Notes

Note: Jesus Christ alone is to be worshipped, but the subject of angels is a very significant subject within the Scriptures. There are over 286 references to angels in the Bible and many of them refer to their interaction with man.

Angels often minister the glory of the Lord because, although they are created beings, they have stood in His presence for thousands of years.

In Bible history we find that God in His sovereignty often chose to send angels with messages and assignments, rather than sending His own Spirit. He even at times delivered prophetic messages to His prophets through angels (see the book of Zechariah). At a very important event (the impregnation of Mary, the mother of Jesus), He used an angel to deliver the message to her. When Mary did not understand the angel's message, it is interesting to note that she asked the angel for understanding concerning the Word, rather than inquiring directly of the Lord.

A. Some Types of Angels Found in Scripture

1. Seraphim —Isaiah 6:1-7

2. Cherubim —Ezekiel 10

3. Zoa (Living Creatures) —Revelation 4:6; 5:14

4. Spirit Horses, Chariot Drivers —2 Kings 2:11-12; 6:13-17; Zechariah 1:8-11

5. Archangels (Chief Princes) —Daniel 10:11-21; 12:1; Revelation 12:7-9

6. Common angels —Matthew 1:20, 24; 2:13, 19

B. General Facts

1. They were created before the earth —Job 38:4-7; Psalm 148:2-5

2. They are not to be worshipped —Colossians 1:16; Revelation 19:10

3. They are innumerable. —Luke 2:13; Hebrews 12:22

4. They are subject to God —Matthew 22:30

C. The Works of Angels

1. Bring answers to prayer —Daniel 9:21-28

2. Minister to the saints —Hebrews 1:14

3. Worship God —Revelation 5:11; Psalm 148:2

4. Carry out God's orders —Psalm 103:20

5. Wage warfare —Revelation 12:7-9; Daniel 10:12-13

6. Watch over children —Matthew 18:10

7. Strengthen people during trials —Matthew 4:11

8. Lead sinners to people who will share the gospel with them —Acts 10:3

9. Direct preachers —Acts 8:26

10. Appear in dreams —Matthew 1:20-24

11. Minister before God —Revelation 8:2; 14:15-19

12. Protect believers from harm —Psalm 91:11; Acts 12:7-10

13. Guard the abyss —Revelation 9:1; 20:1-3

14. Watch over the interest of churches —Revelation 2–3

15. Affect the affairs of nations —Daniel 10:12-13

16. Extraordinary acts —Acts 7:53; 12:6-7; Galatians 3:19

17. Bring God's people special messages —Luke 1

18. Punish God's enemies —Acts 12:23; 2 Samuel 24:16

Lesson Twelve Notes

Lesson Twelve Notes

D. THE NATURE OF ANGELS

1. Intelligent and wise   —2 Samuel 14:20; 19:27; Matthew 24:36

2. Patient   —Numbers 11:22-35

3. Meek   —2 Peter 2:11

4. Joyful   —Luke 15:1-10

5. Modest   —1 Corinthians 11:10

6. Holy   —Mark 8:38

7. Glorious   —Luke 9:26

8. Immortal   —Luke 20:36

9. Mighty, powerful, have great authority   —2 Thessalonians 1:7-10; Revelation 18:1

10. Obedient   —Psalm 103:20

11. Have wills   —Isaiah 14:12-14

12. Are referred to in most cases as "male"   —Judges 13:6; Daniel 10:5-21

    One reference of "female"   —Zechariah 5:5-9

13. Spirit bodies with limbs, eyes, voice, etc.   —Hebrews 13:2; Judges 13:6; Revelation 15:1-6

14. Need no rest   —Revelation 4:8

15. Eat food   —Genesis 18:8; 19:3; Psalm 78:25

16. Can appear visible and invisible   —Numbers 22:35; John 20:12; Hebrews 13:2

17. Can operate in the physical realm   —Genesis 18:1-19; 2 Kings 19:35

18. Can travel at inconceivable speed   —Revelation 8:13; 9:1

Angelic Majesties

19. Can ascend and descend   —Genesis 28:12; John 1:51

20. Can speak languages   —1 Corinthians 13:1

E. Man's Interaction with Angels

1. Ate angel's food   —Psalm 78:25

2. Led Abraham's servant   —Genesis 16:7,9

3. Moses and the burning bush   —Exodus 3:2

4. Gideon   —Judges 6:11-22

5. Elijah was fed and strengthened   —1 Kings 19:5-8

6. David (census)   —1 Chronicles 21:9-27

7. Zechariah   —Zechariah 1:11-14

8. Philip   —Acts 8:26

9. Cornelius   —Acts 10:3-23

10. Peter   —Acts 12:7-11,15

11. Herod   —Acts 12:23

12. Paul   —Acts 27:23

13. John   —Revelation 2–3

Lesson Twelve Notes

LESSON THIRTEEN

THE FIRE

A. BAPTIZED WITH FIRE

Matthew 3:1-12

Acts 1:5; 2

In Matthew 3, we see evidence of three baptisms. The first was baptism in water, which was a baptism unto repentance. The next two were prophesied by John the Baptist concerning Jesus, and they were the baptism with/in/by the Holy Spirit and the baptism with/in/by fire.

The baptism in water was ministered by John, but the other two baptisms were to be ministered by Jesus. In Acts 1:5, Jesus speaks to His disciples and He says, "You will be baptized with the Holy Spirit not many days from now." Notice that He did not say "...with the Holy Spirit *and with fire*." He mentioned only the baptism with the Holy Spirit.

On the day of Pentecost, the Holy Spirit came in power and the Scripture says that "they were all filled with the Holy Spirit." The Scripture does not mention them all being filled with fire.

Lesson Thirteen Notes

The word *baptized* in the Greek is "baptizo" and it actually means to be completely immersed or completely filled. The Scriptures record that the believers were "filled" with the Holy Spirit, but the only evidence of fire on the day of Pentecost was what appeared to be tongues of fire resting on each one (Acts 2:3). This is not baptism (totally immersed or completely filled).

My belief is that the appearance of the tongues of fire was a prophetic foretaste of a corporate "baptism of fire" that is yet to come at the end of the age.

On the day of Pentecost the believers were baptized with the Holy Spirit. This baptism was to provide boldness and power for the disciples to be witnesses for Christ unto the uttermost parts of the earth (Acts 2:8). It was a baptism of empowerment. The work of the gospel continues to spread into every nation through empowered believers.

Now then, what is the baptism with fire for? I believe that this baptism with fire will be given by Jesus at the end of the age for the purifying and glorifying of the church prior to Christ's return.

Of course, there are individuals who have and will continue to experience the glorious fire of God, even as throughout the Old Testament there were many believers who were acquainted with the presence and empowerment of the Holy Spirit. But the corporate empowering of the Holy Spirit did not come until Pentecost. An enormous and glorious corporate outpouring of the baptism of fire is yet to come to His church. In the meantime, any born-again believer can enjoy and experience the fire of God.

B. Different Kinds of Fire

1. The Refiner's Fire   —Malachi 3:1-4

2. The Consuming Fire   —Malachi 4:1-3

3. Fire of Revelation   —Revelation 1:14

4. Illuminating Fire   —Nehemiah 9:15-19; Psalm 105:39

5. Fire of Protection   —Zechariah 2:5

6. Fire of Purging and Consecration   —Isaiah 6:1-8

7. The Fire of Love and Passion   —Song of Songs 8:6-7

C. What the Fire Does

1. Refines and purifies   —Malachi 3:1-4; Matthew 3:11-12

2. Devours the Lord's adversaries   —Psalm 18:8; 97:3; Deuteronomy 9:1-3

3. Convicts hypocrites   —Isaiah 33:10-17

4. Purges believer from sin   —Isaiah 4:2-6; 6:1-8; Jeremiah 23:29

5. Tests our work   —1 Corinthians 3:10-15

6. Gives light   —Exodus 13:21-22

7. Expresses God's wrath/judgment   —Ezekiel 21:31; 22:21, 31; 38:19; Revelation 18

8. Restores the fear of the Lord   —Hebrews 12; Deuteronomy 4:24; Exodus 24:17

9. Ignites believers' hearts with passion   —Acts 2:3-4; Revelation 3:14-22

10. Gives witness to God's presence   —Psalm 39:3

11. Softens and melts   —Psalm 68:2; Ezekiel 22:20

12. Is a wonder   —Exodus 3:1-6

13. Reveals the glory of God   —Isaiah 60:1-3

14. Releases healing   —Malachi 4:1-3

15. Bears witness to Christ's presence   —Luke 24:32

Lesson Thirteen Notes

Lesson Thirteen Notes

D. What Is the Fire?

1. God the Father is the Fire   —Isaiah 30:27-28; Hebrews 12:29

2. Jesus Christ is the Fire   —Ezekiel 1:27; Revelation 1:14-16; Habakkuk 3:4; Acts 9:3

3. The Holy Spirit is the Fire   —Revelation 4:5; Zechariah 2:5

4. Angels manifest as fire   —Psalm 104:4

5. Fire is a manifestation of glory

E. The Fire of God will Have Different Effects on Different People

1. Depends on the condition of their heart

2. Effects wood differently than gold

3. Has a different effect on wax than clay

F. How to Receive the Fire

1. Commit yourself completely to the Lord.

2. Repent from any known and unconfessed sin.

3. Believe.

4. Receive by faith.

5. Soak (just like a candlewick soaks in oil so that it will ignite, so can we soak in the presence of the Holy Spirit by faith).

6. Stay focused.

7. Respond with a thankful heart.

THE FIRE

G. Hindrances to Receiving the Fire

1. Unbelief
2. Lack of understanding on covenant and new creation realities
3. Fear of the unknown
4. Fear of not receiving
5. Jealousy and competition
6. Critical or judgmental attitude
7. Unconfessed sin
8. Lack of consecration to God

Lesson Thirteen Notes

Lesson Fourteen

The Glory

A. What Is the Glory?

Who is God? He is indescribable! His glory is essentially all that He is and all that He does. It means "weight, splendor, copiousness, majesty."

The glory of God manifests in many different ways:

1. The cloud of glory   —Exodus 16:10; 2 Chronicles 5:13-14
2. The fire of glory   —Exodus 3:2; 13:22; 24:17
3. Heavenly glory   —Isaiah 6:1-8; Revelation 1, 4, 5
4. Angelic glory   —Luke 2:13-15
5. Appearance of light and brilliance   —Ezekiel 1:27-28
6. His felt presence   —Exodus 33:14
7. His voice   —Psalm 29:3-9
8. His blessings and goodness   —Exodus 33:18-19
9. Signs and wonders   —Acts 2:19-20

Lesson Fourteen Notes

10. The Father is "the Father of Glory" —Ephesians 1:17

11. Jesus is "The King of Glory" —Psalm 24

12. The Holy Spirit is "the Spirit of Glory" —1 Peter 4:14

B. God Has Always Wanted Man to Partake of His Glory

1. In the beginning (Genesis):

    a. Everything was full of glory (even the dirt that man was made of).

    b. Man was clothed in glory.

    c. Man was made of the dust of "glory particles."

2. Tabernacle (outer, inner court, holy of holies) in the wilderness —Exodus 40:34-38

3. Solomon's Temple —2 Chronicles 5:2,13-14; 7:1-3

4. The glory of the "latter house" —Haggai 2:1-9; Ephesians 5:27; 2 Peter 1:3

5. The last days —Habakkuk 2:14; Zechariah 2:5

6. Back to Genesis —2 Corinthians 4:16-18; 5:1-4

7. Beholding the glory of Jesus —John 17:22-24

C. Glory and the Open Heaven

1. The open heaven —Deuteronomy 28:12

2. God speaks from His glory (i.e. Moses and Peter)

3. The glory protects us —Exodus 14:19-24

4. The glory wins battles —Psalm 24

5. Provision is found in the glory —Philippians 4:19; Haggai 2

6. The glory will transform us   —2 Corinthians 3:17-18

7. Increased visions, dreams, angelic visitations and revelation under the blessing of an open heaven   —Ezekiel 1:1; Revelation 4:1-2; Genesis 28:10-12

8. Visitations of the Holy Spirit   —Matthew 3:16; Acts 10:38

D. Opening Portals of Glory

A "portal" is an opening (door, window, gate or opening) —Psalm 24

1. Obedience   —Deuteronomy 28:1-13

2. Repentance   —Matthew 3; Daniel 9–10

3. Worship and Praise   —2 Chronicles 5

4. Prayer   —2 Chronicles 7:13-14

5. Faith   —Hebrews 11:1

6. Tithes and offerings   —Malachi 3

E. Last Days Outpouring of the Glory

Isaiah 60:1-5

1. Arise, shine; for your light has come.

    Light – fire, flames, light, illumination that comes from fire

2. His glory will ARISE upon believers and APPEAR upon believers   —v. 1-2

3. Great darkness will cover the earth but as this happens the glory will increase.

4. There will be widespread evangelism and harvest.   —v. 3-4

5. People in governmental authority will be saved.   —v. 3

6. Many prodigals will return to the Lord.   —v. 4

Lesson Fourteen Notes

7. There will be great rejoicing among God's people. —v. 5

8. There will be an inversion of wealth. —v. 5

F. How to Receive the Glory

1. Commit yourself completely to the Lord.

2. Repent from any known and unconfessed sin.

3. Believe.

4. Receive by faith.

5. Soak (just like a candlewick soaks in oil so that it will ignite, so can we soak in the presence of the Holy Spirit by faith).

6. Stay focused.

7. Respond with a thankful heart.

G. Hindrances to Receiving the Glory

1. Unbelief

2. Lack of understanding on covenant and new creation realities

3. Fear of the unknown

4. Fear of not receiving

5. Jealousy and competition

6. Critical or judgmental attitude

7. Unconfessed sin

8. Lack of consecration to God

9. Striving

Lesson Fifteen

Heavenly Provision

Your Heavenly Father knows what you have need of and has opened the heavens for you so that you will have more than enough! Believers are called to prosperity! What does prosperity mean? Well, it means that you will always have enough to honor God, enough to meet your own personal needs, and enough left over to help others in their need.

There is no need to fear lack. There is an abundance of resource and provision waiting for you to access – this is part of exploring the heavenly glory.

A. In the Beginning

1. Adam was given dominion over all the earth and everything in it.   —Genesis 1:26

2. Adam was blessed to be fruitful, to multiply, to fill the earth.   —Genesis 1:28

3. God had supplied everything that Adam needed.   —Genesis 1:29

4. Adam was clothed in the glory and he fellowshipped with God.

Lesson Fifteen Notes

B. The Fall and the Curse

1. The ground was cursed.   —Genesis 3:17

2. Man would have to toil and labor in order to bring forth from the earth.   —Genesis 3:17-19

3. Adam had settled for the devil's lies and had chosen the "tree of the knowledge of good and evil" instead of the "tree of life" that was available to him.

C. Restored in Christ

1. In Christ, we have been delivered from sin and its curse and consequences.   —Romans 8:2

2. All the blessings in the heavenly places in Christ are ours.   —Ephesians 1:3

3. In Christ, everything that pertains to life and godliness has already been granted to us.   —2 Peter 1:2-4

4. Christ became poor so that we might be rich. —2 Corinthians 8:9

5. We are to prosper and be in good health as our soul prospers (as our soul understands the provision of God)   —3 John 2

D. Why the Tithe?

1. Honoring God with the first and the best   —Genesis 4:1-5

2. Opens the heavens   —Malachi 3:10-12

3. Overcomes the world and Babylon   —Revelation 18 (teaching to clarify)

4. Abraham and Melchizedek   —Hebrews 7:6-8

E. The Law of Sowing and Reaping

1. Seedtime and harvest —Genesis 8:22

2. Sowing and reaping —2 Corinthians 9: 6-12

3. Good soil —Mark 4:13-20

4. Harvesting is important.

F. Accessing the Blessings by Faith

Review Lesson 4.

In the glory of the Lord is abundance of provision. —Haggai 1-2; Isaiah 60:1-5; Philippians 4:19

G. The Importance of Wisdom

1. In wisdom are riches, honor and long life. —Proverbs 8:18-21

2. Wisdom will teach you management.

H. Know Your Covenant

1. Review Lessons 1 and 2.

2. God gives power to make wealth to confirm His covenant. —Deuteronomy 8:18

I. Hindrances

1. Selfishness restricts the blessings. —James 4:2-4

2. Murmuring and complaining (i.e., Israelites)

3. Unbelief —Hebrews 3–4; James 1:2-8

4. Lack of consecration —Joshua 7

Lesson Fifteen Notes

Lesson Fifteen Notes

5. Disobedience —Hebrews 3, 4

6. Generational curse —Exodus 20:5

Word Confessions for Resource and Provision

I seek first the Kingdom of God and His righteousness, and all these things will be added unto me. I acknowledge that all of my needs are met according to my God's riches in glory by Christ Jesus. I do not fear for it is my Father's good pleasure to give me the Kingdom. Grace and peace are multiplied unto me through the knowledge of God and of Jesus my Lord. His divine power has given me all things that pertain unto life and godliness, through the knowledge of Him that has called me to glory and virtue. Blessed be the God and Father of my Lord Jesus Christ, who has blessed me with every spiritual blessing in the heavenly places in Christ. The Lord is a sun and a shield to me and will give me grace and glory. No good thing will He withhold from me as I walk uprightly. —Matthew 6:33; Philippians 4:19; Luke 12:32; 2 Peter 1:2, 3; Ephesians 1:3; Psalm 84:11

I choose to sow bountifully, therefore I will reap bountifully. I give to the Lord, to His people, and to the needy as I purpose in my heart to give. I do not give grudgingly or out of compulsion, for my God loves a cheerful giver. God makes all grace abound towards me, so that I always have enough for all things, that I may abound unto every good work. The Lord supplies seed for me to sow and bread for my food. He also supplies and multiplies my seed for sowing, and He increases the fruits of my righteousness. I am enriched in everything unto great abundance, which brings much thanksgiving to God. —2 Corinthians 9:6-11

I bring all my tithes into the Lord's storehouse so that there is meat in His house. As a result He opens up the windows of heaven and pours out a blessing for me so that there is not room enough to contain it. He rebukes the devourer for my sake, so that he does not destroy the fruits of my ground and neither does my vine cast its grapes before the time. All the nations shall call me blessed for I shall have a delightful life. I am blessed because I consider the poor. Because I give freely to the poor I will never want. My righteousness endures forever. —Malachi 3:8-12; Psalm 41:1; 112:1,9; Proverbs 28:27

I remember the Lord my God, for it is He who gives me the power to make wealth, that He may confirm His covenant. Because Jesus Christ, my Savior, diligently listened to the voice of God and obeyed all the commandments, the Lord will set me high above all the nations of the earth and all the blessings in the Kingdom shall come upon me and overtake me. Christ became poor so that through His poverty I might become rich. Jesus came so that I would have life in its abundance. —Deuteronomy 8:18; 28:1-2; 2 Corinthians 8:9; John 10:10

APPENDIX

"NUTS, FLAKES, AND WEIRDOS"

from "Third Heaven, Angels, and Other Stuff" by Patricia King

Have you ever attended prayer meetings, church services, or prophetic groups where someone who appeared to be very "spiritual" seemed to create a corporate disruption, leaving people feeling very disturbed? There is a distinct possibility that your meeting was disturbed by a "nut, flake, or weirdo" (from here on referred to as an NFW). However, not all unusual occurrences in meetings are created by NFWs – they could be as a result of a legitimate move of God. When the Holy Spirit moves in power, He often causes some very strange and unique manifestations that might leave some people feeling uncomfortable. God also sometimes causes His people to do strange things for good reasons.

When I think of John the Baptist, I wonder how I would have handled the guy had I lived at that time. My, my! Eating locusts? Yelling out in the wilderness?

What would most of us have done with Isaiah if walking down the street on our way to the market one day we found this so-called "prophet" strutting around naked and barefoot? (see Isaiah 20:2-3) Our reaction

Appendix Notes

may be a little sceptical: "Sure, Isaiah, like we really believe the Lord told you to streak for three years."

And then there's Ezekiel who made little barley cakes mixed with dung (see Ezekiel 4:12-15). Imagine his explanation. "Yeppers, it's the new food for prophets, and God gave me the recipe!"

So, what do we do with all this? How do we discern the difference between an NFW and the real thing? What is the difference between religious delusion and true spiritual encounter?

Any time the Lord does something new in His body, you will discover a pure stream of God's Spirit, and alongside of it you will find the "EX-streams." One of those EX-streams contains fleshly defilement and fanaticism. In another Ex-stream you will find the legalists who persecute and oppose the true stream. This pattern of pure stream and EX-streams is consistent throughout historical revivals and moves of the Spirit.

As we embrace spiritual experience, it is important to discern the true from the false. Leaders need to learn to pastor, mentor and teach their people about the new things God is doing. This process can be messy, uncomfortable and challenging. Sometimes it might seem easier to just "can" the whole thing and shut down the moving of the Spirit.

However, we must not "throw the baby out with the bath water." Think of the scenario of teaching children to eat food on their own. The first time you put the spoon into their little hand, the food seems to go everywhere but in their mouth. They get gravy in their hair, mushed up peas on their T-shirt, and chocolate pudding smeared all over their face, hands, and legs.

They're happy, though — yep, their grin is as big as their face. It takes a lot of extra work to wash their face and hands, shampoo their hair, launder the T-shirt, and clean up the high chair, the floor and any place else where the "food experience" splattered. We could say, "Forget this! I will feed you from now on! You make too much of a mess! The new family rule is that only mom or dad can feed the kids." Oh sure! That might work for a while, but it will look pretty pathetic when you are still hand feeding your twenty-year-old.

Progress, maturity and growth can often be messy. So, too, is the maturing process of something new in the body of Christ. Great discernment, patience, and wisdom are required. In the area of spiritual experiences, heavenly encounters, and angelic visitations there is potential for error. Consequently, good guidelines and scriptural perimeters are necessary. Driving an automobile on a busy street is also dangerous, but it doesn't mean that we should never learn to drive. We simply need to learn the rules of the road, abide by the perimeters set by the law, and proceed with care.

Examining the Fruit

Jesus said that we would know a tree by its fruit. He taught that a good tree would not bear bad fruit and a bad tree would not bear good fruit (see Matthew 7:17-19). I have personally seen many things in the body of Christ over the last number of years that have at times made my hair stand on end. These situations need to be examined and evaluated according to Scripture and the fruit that is evident in a person's life.

What Is Going On in Your Heart?

One test I have found helpful is to ask the person who is being "influenced" what is going on in their heart. God always looks at the heart while man looks at the outward appearance. This is a good place to start. Most of the time, an individual will be able to share with you what the Lord is doing in or through them at the moment. It is good to listen and evaluate according to the plumb line of the Word of God. God is not the author of confusion and, therefore, the response should bring clarity.

Corporate Influence

Another test is to check out the "corporate influence." Is the overall well-being of the meeting disturbed? We have been in sessions where there were some very unusual things transpiring, and yet there was a corporate peace, flow, and witness. At other times, however, there has been unrest in the corporate group (or in individuals) accompanied by a sense of isolated or general disturbance. NFWs are often out-of-the-flow of the corporate anointing. This is a sign that something might be "off" and will need further evaluation and investigation.

Sometimes if a situation has been in question, we will organize a meeting with the person who is manifesting and also with some of those who have been disturbed by it. Many times, through honest dialogue we are able to evaluate and assess the situation better. Good listening skills are important.

It is vital that believers learn to receive confrontation without absorbing rejection. Confrontation, of course, needs to be gentle (although sometimes firm). "The wisdom that is from above is ... easy to be intreated" (see James 3:17).

I remember a particular incident that took place in a prayer group. One of the intercessors was engaging in loud, aggressive, "birthing and travailing" intercession in a meeting where the general flow of the session was not in that vein. Her intercession was extremely disturbing to the rest of the team. When she was invited to join the group in their direction, she explained that she couldn't because the Holy Spirit was leading her in a different way and that she had to complete her intercession. The rest of the prayer team was offended and did not know what to do. The "wailer and travailer" was also offended because she felt restricted, believing she was being unduly restrained from obeying the Holy Spirit.

We brought every member together and heard the heart of each individual involved. They explained how they were feeling at the time and what they sensed the Spirit was saying to them. It helped to hear each other's hearts. Following a time of sharing and prayer they invited the Lord to show them wisdom on how to keep the corporate unity and flow, yet facilitate the wailing and travailing prayer.

It was agreed that if the general flow of the meeting (which was to be determined by the prayer group leader) was not bearing witness to engaging in the birthing prayer, then the wailer and travailer would go into another room to complete her intercession. This would facilitate peace in the general prayer meeting, allowing the members to carry on with an agreed upon corporate flow. At the same time it gave honor and respect to what the wailer and travailer was carrying in her heart. She was in agreement with this.

There was humility and teachability in the hearts of all those individuals. These attributes do not usually accompany NFWs. However, in a case like this, you will want to keep a watch on the situation. If there are subsequent occurrences that create discord or confusion, you might need to do some further investigation. You may possibly have someone in your group that needs some help, mentoring, or healing … or you might have an NFW that is in need of adjustment, discipline, and a whole lot of love!

Drawing Attention to Self?

If an individual within a group is performing acts which draw attention to themselves, then there is room to be concerned. The focus in any spiritual experience should be Jesus, and therefore anything or anyone that would distract from that focus is a possible sign that an NFW is in your midst.

Often there is a sense of the individual in question moving independently from the rest of the group. For instance, sometimes in prayer meetings we find the leader giving direction to the group while an individual will be off in a corner engaged in something totally different. When they are asked to join in with the others, they give some explanation as to how they believe that the Spirit is leading them "differently" and they refuse to join in. There is a sense of separation, lack of submission, distraction, and independence, from the rest of the prayer team. This is often the M.O. of an NFW.

Spiritual Antennas Are Agitated

We have found through experience that most NFWs create a reaction in sensitive prophetic intercessors and others in the body. I remember a situation a few years ago where almost an entire church congregation was negatively stirred in their discernment concerning someone who desired to make this particular house of worship their church family. The spiritual antennas of the leadership team, intercessors, and church

Appendix Notes

family were agitated. This is a sign that something is definitely "off." Jesus said that His sheep would hear His voice and they would not follow the voice of a stranger. He further said that His sheep would actually flee from a stranger (see John 10:4-5). The gift of the discerning of spirits is in believers and will be stirred when things are "not quite right." If there are many who feel uncomfortable, then beware! It is important to heed those checks in the spirit. They are God's warning signals.

When dealing with NFWs, we have at times found that there is strong disagreement and resistance in their hearts towards what leaders are discerning. They will plead their case with Scripture and with explanations that seem to make some sense. As a leader, if after listening with openness to their heart, you still have an uneasy feeling, a check in your spirit, or a subtle caution within, then do not lay down your discernment. Stand in confidence. At times when my discernment has been challenged by an NFW, I have just had to explain, "I might be wrong but at this time I am not comfortable and so I will stand in my discernment for now."

Favor with God and Man

A believer operating in true anointing should be growing in favor with the general body of believers. Jesus grew in favor with God and man (see Luke 2:52). We have often heard an NFW claim that they have a very intimate relationship with the Lord (even deeper than the average believer). They describe their many spiritual experiences and yet they do not have a general or growing favor with the body of Christ. Oftentimes they will claim that this is due to the body being religious and not understanding the "true anointing."

Generally speaking, we find that if a person's horizontal relationships are not bearing fruit then there is more than likely something not quite right with their vertical relationship with God.

Jesus is a great example to us in the way that He related with people in the earth. His vertical relationship with His Heavenly Father could not have been any closer, and you will not find another more "spiritual" than Jesus Himself. Yet, He related very well with those around Him. "He grew in favor with God and man."

Jesus was favored in the temple and the synagogues. We know that there were some in the "religious community" who persecuted Him, but for the most part He was favored in the house of the Lord. He preached in the synagogues and was called "Teacher" and "Rabbi." The sinners also favored Jesus. The multitudes, both sinner and saint, followed Him.

Jesus was very practical and "down to earth" even though He was "heavenly." Sometimes we have found that NFWs have a difficult time relating to the practical dimension of life. It seems as though their head is in the clouds and there is not a clear connection to the natural realm in the earth. Jesus was extremely spiritual and yet very practical. He was so "normal" that some were very amazed at His reputation of being the Son of God, for they said, "Is not this the carpenter's son?" (Matthew 13:55) Jesus was incarnated into the human race and related well to the earthly realm. If we are truly heavenly minded then we will bear fruit in the natural dimension of life. If we are not being any earthly good then perhaps we should question our biblical foundations and spiritual experiences.

OFFENSE AND BITTERNESS

We have further discovered that NFWs often have a root of offense towards the religious authority figures or leaders in the body of Christ.

Offense is extremely dangerous. The moment we sow a seed of critical judgment and offense, we have actually drawn into ourselves the very thing that we have judged and been offended by. I have seen this repeatedly and consistently. Many NFWs have roots of offense and bitter judgments in their lives that have stemmed from some wounding from the past. We have found that often they have trust issues that need to be healed.

A reservoir of water might be completely pure, however the water that comes out of the tap will be defiled if there is rust in the pipe through which the water travels from the original source. This is how it works in the realm of the spirit as well. A believer has a pure pool of living water within them but if there is offense, bitterness, unhealed hurts, and judgments in their soul, then the gifts and blessings of the Lord will not be released in purity. The "rust" will defile the water.

Folks can get sick by drinking bad water. We have seen negative effects on those who have allied themselves with NFWs. Some pastors have testified that they have experienced NFWs sowing discord and dissension into their entire church family.

True spiritual believers walk in a heart of unity with the rest of the body and demonstrate a submissive spirit especially to those in authority. They do not walk in or breed an independent attitude.

There are times when we might feel a strong conviction regarding something that differs from the teachings of our spiritual leaders or others in the body. It is healthy to discuss these differences with a heart of honesty and truth and yet with utmost humility, respect, and honor. We must always remain teachable.

When we are entering into spiritual experience, it is important that we are willing to be challenged by those who do not understand. Confrontation and challenge is healthy for us and will perfect and refine that which we believe. If our experience is truly from God, it will stand the test of the Word and the nature and character of God. This is part of being teachable and growing and maturing. NFWs often do not like to be challenged, and instead of being open they become defensive during times of confrontation.

It is imperative that every believer has a strong circle of accountability around his or her life. Recently we were dealing with an individual who felt they had received some specific direction from the Lord for their future. They had received this direction from spiritual vision and revelatory experience. A number of mature Christians and leaders around her had very strong concerns and communicated that they felt she was in deception. She stood against their counsel and claimed that they didn't understand her call. She believed her call was on a higher level than what they understood. This is dangerous and life-threatening thinking!

DECEPTION, PRIDE AND LEVIATHAN

Deception is going to increase in the last days, and it is important that we understand the dangers (see 2 Thessalonians 2:9-10; 1 Timothy 4:1-2,16; 2 Timothy 3:1-5,13; Matthew 24:4-5,11). Usually you will find an NFW in some level of error in their doctrinal or theological interpretations.

A love for truth will help keep you from deception. There are times as Christians that we might be touched by deception, but we can trust the Lord to deliver us if we have a love for truth.

When I was on a mission field a number of years ago, I was working with some leaders who were deceived by legalism. They believed that in order to please the Lord and to have relationship with Him you had to really work at perfecting your life. They would often point out things in my life that they believed were offensive to the Lord and demanded that I "bring things into line." These leaders were very zealous and they genuinely loved the Lord, but they were deceived. At that point in my life, I did not know how to rightly divide the Word in that area, so I bought into the lie. I worked, struggled, and wrestled in order to bring my flesh into subjection, only to find that I couldn't perfect it. The pressure of all this self-effort left me desolate. I had been deceived.

On my return home, my church leaders pointed out to me the error I had entered into and they helped me walk out of it. I was hungry for truth. When they spoke the truth to me, I recognized it. I had many questions as I journeyed through the healing process, but the Lord honored my love for truth. Truth is a Person – Truth is Jesus. The Word is also truth. In John 17:17, the Scripture says, "Sanctify them in the truth; Your word is truth." That taste of deception immunized me from that point on. I can now "smell a legalistic spirit a mile away." All things work together for good. Peter was deceived when he denied Christ, and yet when he came through it he became a valuable apostolic servant in the Kingdom of God. Jesus prayed that his "faith may not fail" (see Luke 22:32).

The leaders on the mission field made a mistake, and their choices caused pain in my life. It was important for me to forgive them and to

Appendix Notes

continue to honor them. We all make mistakes and we all hurt people from time to time even when we are not intending to. It is important to show mercy instead of judgment when you are hurt. Our areas of pain can become to us a stumbling block or a stepping stone in our life depending on how we handle the situation.

It is very wise to submit spiritual revelations and interpretations of the Word to an accountability circle of respected leaders to ensure safety. I know of many who have taken the Word, quoted it, and applied it to their lives in deceptive ways. Submission to their leaders for doctrinal accountability would have most likely kept them from error.

Pride is often in the root system of an NFW. Pride is extremely dangerous and can often find a place in a person's life through fear of rejection or failure. It is a defense mechanism that has brought many to ruin. An evil spirit that attaches itself to the sin of pride in believers is the deadly spirit of Leviathan. In Job 41 we find a detailed description of the operations of this evil spirit. Leviathan is referred to in this chapter as the "king over all the sons of pride" (v. 34). In verse 15 it says that Leviathan's scales are its pride. In verse 26 of Job 41, the Scripture says that even the sword cannot take him out. In Scripture the "sword" is symbolic of the Word of God. We have found in our dealings with some NFWs that when we bring the Word to point out their error, they will often twist its interpretation, or they will talk around the issue. The key to freedom is an absolute commitment to humility. Humility will take out Leviathan. Moving in the opposite spirit to pride is so essential.

If pride is not repented of and replaced by the standard of humility then an NFW has the potential to cause many problems in church community. We have literally seen this "twisted serpent" (Leviathan spirit) attempt to take out entire congregations. It is brutal and very dangerous. Individuals who will not submit to the Word, to authority, or to discipline in a spirit of humility are in danger of walking in terrible deception as well as leading others into it. In cases like this, the individual might need to be released from the prayer group or church.

Philippians 2:1-8 describes the attitude and heart that true spiritual believers should walk in. It describes humility, servanthood, esteeming others, and walking in obedience; it calls us to have these attitudes in ourselves. 2 Timothy 2:24 describes the attitude of God's true servants by saying, "The Lord's bond-servant must not be quarrelsome, but be kind to all." As we walk in these values we will grow in favor with God and man. If our ways please the Lord, He will cause even our enemies to be at peace with us (see Proverbs 16:7).

You might be wondering at this point, "Oh no! Am I a nut, flake or weirdo"? Well, why don't you pray and ask the Lord if there is anything in your heart that might need to be adjusted. If so – well, then, simply make the adjustment. You are a loved and precious child of God.

Others of you might be thinking, "Oh ya! I know a few of those NFWs." Well, for you I might ask these questions: "What can you do to help them be all that God wants them to be?" Will you commit yourself to them in prayer or perhaps through counseling, loving confrontation, discipline and mentoring? Are you willing to get to know their heart? And finally, have you examined your own heart to search it for judgmental, critical and condescending attitudes? Just maybe you too are an NFW and didn't know it! It is so important that we do not stand in critical judgment towards anyone and yet walk in great discernment during these days.

The Kingdom is all about love, His love. And you know what? He loves us all – even if we are a bit nutty, flaky and even weird at times. He loves us enough to discipline us and lead us into adjustment. Are we willing to walk the processes through with Him? Are we willing to walk the processes through with others?

The passion of the Lord is to see His children living in the fullness of heavenly blessings. Third heaven, angels and all kinds of other stuff are awaiting us in Him. But more than anything, He wants us to experience the fullness of His love for Him and for each other. Wow, what an invitation to come up higher!

Are you up for it?

PATRICIA KING

Patricia is president of both Extreme Prophetic and Christian Services Association. She has been a pioneering voice in ministry, with over 30 years of background as a Christian minister in conference speaking, prophetic service, church leadership, and television & radio appearances. Patricia has written numerous books, produced many CDs and DVDs, hosts Extreme Prophetic TV, and is the CEO of a popular online media network – XPmedia.com. Patricia's reputation in the Christian community is world-renowned.

Christian Services Association (CSA) was founded in Canada in 1973 and in the USA in 1984. It is the parent ministry of Extreme Prophetic, a 501-C3 founded in 2004 in Arizona. CSA/Extreme Prophetic is located in Maricopa, AZ and Kelowna, B.C. Patricia King and numerous team members equip the body of Christ in the gifts of the Spirit, prophetic ministry, intercession, and evangelism. CSA/Extreme Prophetic is called to spreading the gospel through media.

Author Contact Information

Extreme Prophetic/CSA
U.S. Ministry Center
P.O. Box 1017
Maricopa, AZ 85139

XP Canada Ministry Center
3054 Springfield Road
Kelowna, B.C V1X 1A5
CANADA

Telephone: 1-250-765-9286
E-mail: info@XPmedia.com

Other Books and Resources by Patricia King

All listed resource is available at the XPmedia Bookstore.
www.XPmedia.com

Decree the Word!

Decree a thing and it shall be established. Job 22:28

Decree by Patricia King. The Word of God is powerful and it will profoundly influence your life. It does not return void, but accomplishes everything that it is sent to do. This book helps believers activate the power of the Word in key areas of their lives, including health, provision, love, victory, wisdom, family, business, spiritual strength and many others.

This expanded, revised edition features new decrees, including glory, blessing, favor, and prayer.

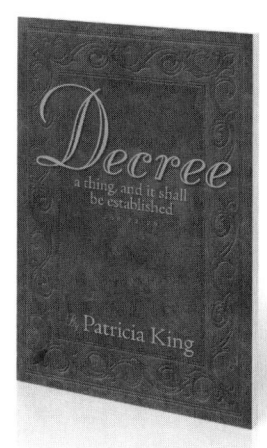

Decree CD. Patricia King speaks forth many of the decrees that are in the Decree book. Heather Clark accompanies with powerful music. When declarations of the Word are proclaimed over you, the Word is then activated to strengthen your spirit man and prepare you for every good Kingdom work.

Worship and Decrees that Soak You in His Purifying Presence!

The Spiritual Cleanse, soaking CD by Patricia King, is full of prayers and decrees written and proclaimed by Patricia King, accompanied by worship music from Steve Swanson. As you listen, you will be soaked in the purifying presence of the Living Word of God.

It's like taking time off and going to a "spiritual spa"! Let the power of the blood of Jesus Christ gently wash over you, as you receive a deep spiritual cleanse.

Other Books and Resources by Patricia King

All listed resource is available at the XPmedia Bookstore.
www.XPmedia.com

Walk in Wholeness and Freedom!

The School of Deliverance, 8 CD set and manual by Patricia King. Do you suffer with guilt, shame, emotional pain, addictive behavior, irrational fears or rejection? Are you trapped by past failures or generational bondage?

The School Of Deliverance introduces you to realms of healing and deliverance as Patricia King teaches, preaches, and prophesies you into new-found freedom. Wounds of the past will be healed, and oppressive powers will be broken over lives. You can walk in wholeness and freedom. And you can minister it to others!

Step into the BLESSING ZONE!

You were created to be blessed, to know the very best that God has to offer all the days of your life. If you have been living in a place of lack, hardship, or frustration, it is time to shift into the Blessing Zone and know the goodness of God in every area of your life!

In this powerful new book, Patricia King shares divine secrets of how you can step out of simply living day-to-day and live IN THE ZONE!

Drink of the revelation of His Love!

This booklet by Patricia King is designed to introduce you to the greatest revelation anyone could ever receive. It is the revelation of God's unconditional love for you – the love that was perfectly tested and proven at the cross, 2,000 years ago. Drink deeply of this revelation and come to the full realization that God Loves You with an Everlasting Love!

Other Books and Resources by Patricia King

All listed resource is available at the XPmedia Bookstore.
www.XPmedia.com

Join the Spiritual Revolution!

This book will shake the way you think about the supernatural power of God – and your role in combatting the counterfeit signs and wonders of today's cults. It contains stories, insights and practical suggestions about how you can aggressively choose to live in the supernatural power of God.

Enlist in the *Spiritual Revolution* and you will be transformed into a powerful witness throughout an eternal lifetime!

You are meant to be a light in this world!

Is your heart's cry to be used mightily by the Lord? Do you want to shine God's goodness in this dark, decaying world? Are you hungry to move out, seeing miracles and salvations on the streets? Patricia King's book, *Light Belongs in the Darkness*, will set you on fire to be a conduit of Kingdom purposes!

You are meant to be a light in this world. And light belongs in the darkness!

Don't Stop Before You are Finished!

Life does not end at 40, 60, or 80 – it flourishes and gains momentum as you recognize the destiny God designed for all of your days. All the hard lessons you learned in the first half of your life serve as a springboard for the fulfillment of your dreams in the second half!

In *Dream Big*, author Patricia King debunks the myth that only the youthful are relevant in the world.

Start today living the better half of life!

Other Books and Resources by Patricia King

All listed resource is available at the XPmedia Bookstore.
www.XPmedia.com

Break this Destructive Pattern!

In this book Patricia King delves into the psychological and spiritual roots of narcissism, a disorder that is running rampant in both the word and the church. As you read *Overcoming the Spirit of Narcissism*, you will learn what narcissism is and how it manifests, how it takes root in an individual, the truth about narcissism in the church today, how to live with someone who is under of influence of a spirit of narcissism, and much more! A must read!

A Call to The Bride!

Our Father has chosen a very special bride for His Beloved Son – you! In this book Patricia shares insights from Scripture and Hebrew wedding traditions to help you understand Jesus' all-consuming love for you and how to prepare yourself to be His Bride! It is a message to each of us individually, as well as to the church.

Are You Prepared?

The Prayer Shield, 2 CD set by Patricia King. As we move to greater levels of glory and empowerment, we also move to greater levels of resistance and attack. This is nothing to fear, but it is something we must be aware of ... and prepared for. In this teaching, Patricia King shares divine insights and powerful strategies on how to create a fortress of prayer around yourself and others. As you listen, you will receive revelation and impartation to create a mighty and effective PRAYER SHIELD.

Other Books and Resources by Patricia King

All listed resource is available at the XPmedia Bookstore.
www.XPmedia.com

Increase your Prayer Power!

Increase your Prayer Power. This 4 CD teaching by Patricia King will open your eyes and bolster your faith, helping you to step into the full authority the Lord has given to all believers. You will learn principles of prayer, how to stand on the promises of God, and how to receive decrees of the Lord to see breakthrough in any situation you or your loved ones may be facing. Don't limit your Kingdom effectiveness. Begin increasing your prayer power today!

Discover this Powerful Key!

The Power of Honor, 2 CD set by Rob Packer. In this powerful series Rob Packer shows how honor is the key that releases the Church to be who they are supposed to be. It is also the key that releases God to be who He is. You will discover who you really are, how Jesus answers the deepest cry of your heart and how to live in a relationship with God that releases His manifest presence in your life and in the world around you. The world is crying out for the reality of God to be seen. Let Him be seen in you through honor!

See into the Unseen Realm!

Eyes that See. Have you desired to see into the unseen realm? In this small book, Patricia shares how in Christ you have been offered spiritual sight that will enable you to behold Him and the glory of His heart and Kingdom. You have been given "eyes that see!"

Other Books and Resources by Patricia King

All listed resource is available at the XPmedia Bookstore.
www.XPmedia.com

Encounter the Sevenfold Spirit of God!

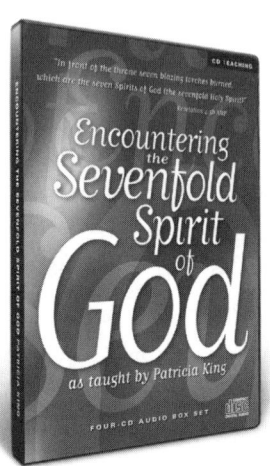

Encountering the Sevenfold Spirit of God, 4-CD set by Patricia King. This teaching was revealed to Patricia during prayer time with the Lord. Learn all that the Holy Spirit has for us and how to access it. This teaching is an open door to more wisdom, revelation, understanding, counsel, might, reverence and anointing. Subjects dealt with include: "Who is the Holy Spirit," "The Sevenfold Spirit of God," "The Seven Dimensions," "How to Encounter the Holy Spirit."

Where Is Your Focus?

Whatever you focus on, you empower. This revelation will launch you into a life filled with dreams coming true! The key is to move beyond hearing into receiving, and then stepping out into the revelation of what you have seen, being confident God will bring it about as you trust in Him and go for it. There is not a promise or blessing of God you cannot have. There is not a mantle or assignment you cannot take up, if you direct your focus and release your passion!

Receive the Powerful Gift of the Spirit!

Patricia King gives an in-depth teaching on the gift of tongues. This will give you both a solid biblical principle on this gift, and an understanding on how to receive it!

Many more resources are available at the bookstore at www.XPmedia.com, including books, teaching sets in CD, DVD and MP3s, music and more. Many resources are downloadable. Check them out!

Additional copies of this book and other book titles from Patricia King, Extreme Prophetic and XP Publishing are available at the store at XPmedia.com

BULK ORDERS: We have bulk/wholesale prices for stores and ministries. Please contact: usaresource@xpmedia.com.

For Canadian bulk orders please contact: resource@xpmedia.com or call 250-765-9286.

www.XPpublishing.com
A Ministry of Patricia King and Christian Services Association